Layman's Bible Book Commentary
Romans, 1 Corinthians

LAYMAN'S BIBLE BOOK COMMENTARY

ROMANS, 1 CORINTHIANS

VOLUME 20

J. W. MacGorman

BROADMAN PRESS
Nashville, Tennessee

© Copyright 1980 • Broadman Press
All rights reserved.

4211-90

ISBN: 0-8054-1190-9

Dewey Decimal Classification: 227.1

Subject headings: BIBLE. N. T. ROMANS//BIBLE. N. T. 1 CORINTHIANS

Library of Congress Catalog Card Number: 79-51501

Printed in the United States of America

To Ruth,
my wife,
joint heir of the grace
of life
(1 Peter 3:7)

Foreword

The *Layman's Bible Book Commentary* in twenty-four volumes was planned as a practical exposition of the whole Bible for lay readers and students. It is based on the conviction that the Bible speaks to every generation of believers but needs occasional reinterpretation in the light of changing language and modern experience. Following the guidance of God's Spirit, the believer finds in it the authoritative word for faith and life.

To meet the needs of lay readers, the *Commentary* is written in a popular style, and each Bible book is clearly outlined to reveal its major emphases. Although the writers are competent scholars and reverent interpreters, they have avoided critical problems and the use of original languages except where they were essential for explaining the text. They recognize the variety of literary forms in the Bible, but they have not followed documentary trails or become preoccupied with literary concerns. Their primary purpose was to show what each Bible book meant for its time and what it says to our own generation.

The Revised Standard Version of the Bible is the basic text of the *Commentary*, but writers were free to use other translations to clarify an occasional passage or sharpen its effect. To provide as much interpretation as possible in such concise books, the Bible text was not printed along with the comment.

Of the twenty-four volumes ot the *Commentary*, fourteen deal with Old Testament books and ten with those in the New Testament. The volumes range in pages from 140 to 168.Four major books in the Old Testament and five in the New are treated in one volume each. Others appear in various combinations. Although the allotted space varies, each Bible book is treated as a whole to reveal its basic message with some passages getting special attention. Whatever plan of Bible study the reader may follow, this *Commentary* will be a valuable companion.

Despite the best-seller reputation of the Bible, the average survey of Bible knowledge reveals a good deal of ignorance about it and its primary meaning. Many adult church members seem to think that its study is intended for children and preachers. But some of the newer translations have been making the Bible more readable for all ages. Bible study has branched out from Sunday into other days of the week, and into neighborhoods rather than just in churches. This *Commentary* wants to meet the growing need for insight into all that the Bible has to say about God and his world and about Christ and his fellowship.

BROADMAN PRESS

Contents

ROMANS

1 CORINTHIANS

ROMANS

Introduction

By every measurement Paul's letter to the church at Rome, the letter we are about to study, is one of the most important ever written. Indeed from a Christian viewpoint many would classify it as the greatest letter of all time.

Several considerations support this lofty estimate. For one, Romans has as author one of the most committed of all men, the apostle Paul. No one in the early churches or since has ever exceeded him in love for Jesus Christ, the Son of God. Furthermore, its message is the grandest of all themes, namely, the grace of God. No New Testament writer ever experienced that grace more dramatically or proclaimed it more faithfully than Paul.

No wonder then that throughout Christian history Romans has played an important role in times of great spiritual renewal. Again and again God has spoken to men at the level of their deepest need through its message. And our earnest prayer is that he may continue to do so during the present study.

Since God's revelation never takes place in a historical vacuum, let us take a few moments to become better acquainted with Paul and his readers. Then we shall be better equipped to understand God's message to them.

The Writer

Several evidences affirm that Paul was the author of this letter. In Romans 1:1 the writer introduced himself as "Paul, a servant of Jesus Christ." Again, in Romans 11:13 he identified himself as "an apostle to the Gentiles." And in the lengthy description of travel plans and personal greetings at the end of the letter (15:14 to 16:27), there are details that fit what we have learned about Paul in other sources. For example, the passage describes Paul's involvement with the Gentile churches in sending a relief offering to the poor believers in Jerusalem (compare Rom. 15:25-27 with Galatians 2:10; 1 Cor. 16:1-4; 2 Cor. 8:1 to 9:15).

And it refers to his prior associations with Priscilla and Aquila (compare Rom. 16:3-5 with Acts 18:2-3,18,26; 1 Cor. 16:19). These evidences point unmistakably to the apostle Paul as the author of Romans, a conclusion that finds strong support in the writings of the church fathers. According to Romans 16:22 Paul used Tertius as a secretary.

But what about Paul the man? We encounter him first as a persecutor of the early Christians. It was at his feet that the men laid their garments in preparation for the stoning of Stephen (Acts 7:58). And in the fierce persecution that followed, Paul sought to destroy the church of God (Acts 8:3; Gal. 1:13-14,23; 1 Cor. 15:9; Phil. 3:6; 1 Tim. 1:13). He did not believe that Jesus was God's Messiah and regarded all who did as enemies of the true faith of Israel. Indeed, Paul was bound for Damascus on a persecuting mission when the risen Lord confronted him and changed his life completely.

The details usually associated with this experience are not found in the main autobiographical passages of Paul's letters (Gal. 1:11 to 2:14; 2 Cor. 11:22 to 12:10; and Phil. 3:4-11). Rather they are found in three accounts of his conversion and call in the book of Acts: 9:1-25; 22:1-21; and 26:1-23. However these passages confirm the testimony of Paul's letters that the exalted Lord arrested him in full persecuting stride and called him to be an apostle to the Gentiles. By the grace of God the arch-persecutor of the early churches became a faithful proclaimer of the gospel. And the change was so dramatic and complete that even Paul recorded the believers' gratitude to God for it (Gal. 1:24).

His Readers

Romans 1:7 reads, "To all God's beloved in Rome, who are called to be saints." Thus we know that the letter was directed to the Christians in Rome. However, nothing in it provides information about the origin of Christian work in the city.

The following theories have been proposed: (1) About AD 185 Irenaeus stated that the Roman church was "founded and organized at Rome by the two most glorious Apostles Peter and Paul. . . . The blessed apostles, then, having founded and built up the Church, committed into the hands of Linus the office of the episcopate."[1] Yet the letter itself bears evidence that Paul was writing to a church he had neither founded nor visited (1:8-15; 15:14-33). Moreover if Peter had been serving as bishop of Rome, Paul would have included him among the many to whom he sent greetings at the end of his letter (16:3-16,21-23). (2) Another theory cites the reference to "visitors from Rome, both Jews and proselytes" at Pentecost in Acts 2:10. Presumably some of these were converted and returned to Rome to establish a church. However, evidence to support the claim is wanting. (3) Still another theory maintains that the church in Rome was established by converts who moved to the imperial city. Some students of the Bible point to the long list of names in chapter 16 as proof that many of these persons were Paul's converts. Yet others use the same evidence to support the claim that this chapter was originally a letter of commendation for Phoebe to the church at Ephesus.[2] All three proposals are little more than interesting speculations, while the origin of the Roman church remains an unresolved historical question.

But we do have reason to believe that the gospel reached Rome at a relatively early date. Acts 18:1-3 describes the banishment of Priscilla and Aquila from Rome, along with all other Jews, during the reign of Claudius (AD 41-54). According to the Roman historian Suetonius, the banishment occurred in the ninth year of his reign (AD 49). Disturbances in the Jewish quarters of the city over the Christian claim that Jesus was the Christ likely caused the edict. If this is so, the witness of the gospel had reached Rome at least by this date and probably earlier.

This claim receives further support in Romans 1:8, where Paul paid a tribute to the widespread influence of the Roman church throughout the Mediterranean world. This presupposes a significant history of the church at the time Romans was written, less than a decade after the banishment.

At this point in our discussion some consideration also needs to be given to the makeup of the congregation. That is, were the members of the church in Rome primarily Jewish or Gentile believers? Some passages suggest that Paul's readers were primarily Jewish. For example, Romans 4:1 speaks of Abraham as "our forefather according to the flesh." Romans 7:1-25 and 8:1-39 contrast the former state under the law with the present condition under grace. And Romans 9:1 to 11:36 focuses upon the problem of Israel's rejection.

However, on balance other passages seem to require the conclusion that Paul's readers were primarily Gentile converts. In Romans 1:5-7,13-15 Paul numbered the church at Rome among the Gentile churches. In Romans 11:13 he addressed his readers as Gentiles and proceeded to warn them against boasting "over the branches" (v. 18), the Jews who had been broken off because of their unbelief (11:20). In Romans 15:14-16 he included the Romans among the Gentiles whom he, as a priest, was offering up to God. Furthermore, most of the persons greeted in chapter 16 have Greek or Latin names.

Date of the Letter

Romans 15:25-29 reveals that Paul wrote the letter shortly before his departure for Jerusalem with the relief offering from the Gentile churches. This fact makes Corinth the most probable place of writing and suggests a date around AD 55-56.

At one time Paul had been undecided about accompanying the delegates from the churches with the offering (1 Cor. 16:4). However, later as the project gained momentum (2 Cor. 8—9), he began to feel a greater compulsion to go. By the time of the Roman letter he had made up his mind. He would go, though he knew that he risked his life by returning to Jerusalem. At an earlier time men there had tried to kill him (Acts 9:28-29), and nothing had happened since then to lessen their hatred.

His decision to lead the Gentile delegation to Jerusalem with the relief offering not only placed his life in jeopardy but also delayed even further his plans to visit Rome and evangelize Spain (1:13; 15:22-29). Why did Paul take such a chance? The answer must be that he felt his presence was necessary to achieve the ultimate goal of unity between Jewish and Gentile Christians. And this goal of unity among the established churches of the East bore directly upon the success of his proposed plan to establish new churches in the West.

Purpose

Paul stated his purpose in a rather low-key fashion in Romans 15:14-15. In the former verse he expressed confidence in the integrity and knowledge of his readers. They were fully capable of instructing one another. Then he added in verse 15, "But on some points I have written to you very boldly by way of reminder."

And what a reminder he has given! The "some points" that he referred to covered the whole range of man's sinfulness (1:18 to 3:20) and God's provision of salvation through faith in Jesus Christ (3:21 to 8:39). They included a discussion of Israel's destiny and the problem of reconciling God's election of Israel with her rejection of the gospel (9—11). They contained a call to Christian commitment (12:1-2) and spelled out its implications for several important issues of discipleship (12:3 to 15:13). Included among these issues were the mounting tensions between Jewish and Gentile believers in Rome over their differences in religious scruples (14:1 to 15:13). Willi Marxsen suggests that these tensions became increasingly acute following the death of Claudius (AD 54), as Jewish believers began to return to Rome.[3]

Whatever Paul's reasons were for minimizing his purpose in writing to the Romans, his letter to them contains his fullest statement of the gospel. How shall we account for the difference in stature between his stated intention in writing and his actual production?

The reason may be found in the references to his forthcoming visit to Rome. In Romans 1:10-13 Paul had mentioned his long-delayed plans to visit the church there. He yearned both to impart and to receive spiritual strength as they shared their mutual faith. However, in Romans 15:22-29 Paul revealed a further insight regarding his plans, namely, his intention to evangelize Spain. To be sure he yearned to be refreshed for a while in the company of the Roman believers (15:24,32), but Rome was not to be his final destination. He felt compelled to launch a new phase of his missionary labors by pressing beyond Rome to Spain, and he needed the support of the Roman church in this venture. Earlier the church at Antioch had provided support for the evangelization of the areas around the Aegean Sea. Now, feeling that his work in the East was drawing to a close, he wanted to enlist Rome's backing for his mission to Spain. Paul may have written Romans as a preparation for his intended Roman visit, feeling that if he were going to ask the Roman Christians to support his mission to Spain he should explain the heart of his teaching, the message he would be taking with him.

Paul's forthcoming trip to Jerusalem with its prospects of further trouble with the unbelieving Jews also has significance for the Roman letter. The possibility of conflict accounts for the grace versus law discussion in a letter addressed to a church whose members were primarily Gentiles. Rome needed to hear what Paul had to say on this vital theme. He knew enough about them, possibly through Priscilla and Aquila (Acts 18:1-4; Rom. 16:3-5) or unspecified reports, to realize that his words were not wasted on them. As he wrote, he knew that Jerusalem also needed to hear what he had to say, as well as all other churches

Salutation

1:1-17

Paul, a Servant of Jesus Christ (1:1-7)

When we write a letter we put the name of the addressee at the beginning and our own at the end. However, in Paul's day it was done differently. Then the writer placed his name first, the identity of his reader or readers next, and also attached a greeting. Furthermore in our salutations we usually are content to state the barest details about ourselves and our readers. And our greeting may be no more than a "Dear John" or "Dear friends." At these points too, there were differences, for the ancient letter writer often expanded the references to himself, his correspondents and his greetings in such a way as to enhance his purpose in writing.

Keep in mind that in Romans Paul was writing to a church he had neither founded nor visited. Other churches such as those in Galatia, Philippi, Thessalonica, and Corinth, had known him as founding apostle or father, but Rome had not. Understandably then, at the beginning of his letter Paul sought to establish his *apostolic authority*. In verse 1 he presented himself as "Paul, a servant of Jesus Christ, called to be an apostle, set apart for the gospel of God." What a remarkable self-introduction this is! Formerly his zeal for the ancestral traditions had brought him honor and advancement within the ranks of Judaism (Gal. 1:13-14). But now he described himself as Christ's bondslave. He testified that God had called him to be an apostle and had set him apart for the work of his gospel. Going forth under divine commission he sought "to bring about the obedience of faith for the sake of his name among all the nations" (v. 5). This included the Romans (v. 6).

Remember, also, Paul's hopes of enlisting Rome's support for the evangelization of Spain, which he would not disclose until near the end of his letter (15:22-29). Equally understandable then was Paul's immediate desire to verify his *apostolic message*. In verse 2 he stated that God had promised his gospel earlier "through his prophets in the holy scriptures." In keeping with other early Christians, Paul saw in the gospel the fulfillment of God's promises in the Old Testament. In verses 3-4 he centered the gospel in Jesus Christ, God's Son. Two great affirmations regarding him were made: (1) With respect to his fleshly existence or incarnation, he was descended from David (v. 3). Several New Testa-

ment passages bear witness to the Davidic descent of Jesus (see Matt.
1:1; Luke 1:31-33; Acts 2:29-30; Rev. 5:5). (2) With respect to his
present status or exaltation, he was designated "Son of God in power
according to the Spirit of holiness by his resurrection from the dead,
Jesus Christ our Lord" (v. 4).

An early Christian creed possibly underlies the affirmations in verses
3-4. Here the emphasis does not fall upon two natures in Christ, human
and divine. Rather it falls upon two stages or events in his life: his
fleshly descent or incarnation and his exaltation in power through the
resurrection.

Thus in the opening lines of his letter to the Romans, Paul introduced
himself as an apostle to the Gentiles. He described the gospel of God in
a way that assured them the gospel he preached was the same one they
believed. And in verse 7 he addressed them as "all God's beloved in
Rome who are called to be saints." Through their faith in Jesus Chrst,
they had been set apart as God's own people.

A benediction both combines and elaborates upon customary Greek
and Jewish greetings: "Grace to you and peace from God our Father
and the Lord Jesus Christ" (v. 7). For the Greek greeting was a word
remarkably similar to the word translated *grace,* and the Jewish greeting (*shalom*) was the word for *peace.* Basic to this benediction is the
insight that the peace of God is known only through the experience of
the grace of God. To look for peace in any other direction is to be on the
wrong track from the beginning. For this reason we can never know the
peace that God is able to give until we experience the grace that God is
eager to bestow.

Thanksgiving and Prayer Request (1:8-15)

Again, in keeping with the ancient letter form, Paul continued his
opening remarks with expressions of thanksgiving and prayer in his
readers' behalf. First, he thanked God for the widespread influence of
their faith (v. 8; compare 1 Thess. 1:8). As observed earlier, this statement provides evidence of a well-established gospel work in Rome preceding the writing of this letter. Rome was the capital of one of the
greatest empires of all time, and it meant much to all believers every-
where that a faithful Christian witness had been planted there.

Then Paul assured his readers that he prayed for them continuously.
Note how often in his letters that Paul reminded his readers that he was
praying for them (compare 1 Thess. 1:2-3; 3:9-10; 1 Cor. 1:4; Phil.

1:3-11). Also, he usually asked his readers to pray for him (Rom. 15:30-33; 1 Thess. 5:25; 2 Cor. 1:11; Phil. 1:19). Thus believers who had never met could be bound together in common prayer.

The substance of Paul's prayer is revealed in the verses that follow (vv. 10-15). For a long time Paul had desired to visit Rome, but something had always intervened to make it impossible (vv. 10,13). Two reasons were given for his longing to see them: (1) He wanted to share some spiritual blessing that would strengthen them (v. 11). The Holy Spirit alone is the sovereign bestower of all spiritual or charismatic gifts (1 Cor. 12:11). However, as one exercises the gifts entrusted to him, the entire church benefits (1 Cor. 12:7). Lest Paul sound as though he regarded himself as giver only, he quickly added his expectations of benefit through the mutual sharing of their faith (v. 12). In Christian service no one is ever completely giver or receiver only. (2) He wanted to participate in the gospel harvest in Rome, even as elsewhere among the Gentiles. Paul applied the harvest metaphor to Christian service or growth in several passages (1 Cor. 9:11; 2 Cor. 9:6; Gal. 6:7-9).

Paul acknowledged himself a debtor "both to Greeks and to barbarians, both to the wise and to the foolish" (v. 14). The term "barbarians" was used by Greeks to designate those who did not speak the Greek language. Thus Paul used broad categories, both ethnic and cultural, to describe the range of the mission to which he was committed. And he expressed an eagerness to preach the gospel in Rome (v. 15).

Theme: the Righteousness of God (1:16-17)

But what is the gospel that Paul was so eager to preach in Rome? Already in his opening remarks he had introduced two important features of the gospel: (1) It is the fulfillment of God's promises through his prophets in the Holy Scriptures (1:2); (2) It centers in the person of Jesus Christ, God's Son and our risen Lord (1:3-4). Here Paul added another feature: The gospel "is the power of God for salvation to every one who believes, to the Jew first and also to the Greek" (v. 16; author's translation).

What is the gospel able to accomplish? The answer is salvation, a concept that lies at the heart of God's purpose for his people, both in the Old and the New Testaments. The term presupposes peril or bondage, that from which men need to be delivered or rescued. And the first major division of the Roman letter (1:18 to 3:20) will make plain that from which we need to be delivered, namely, our sins and the present evil age of which they are an expression.

The good news of the gospel is that Jesus Christ has come into this evil age and by his death and resurrection has made possible our deliverance from it. Through faith in him all men, Jew and Gentile alike, may experience now the salvation whose full deliverance awaits the last day.[4]

In the gospel God reveals his righteousness, and this quality is not a static attribute but a dynamic power. That is, God reveals his righteousness by putting men right with himself through faith in Jesus Christ, his Son. The gospel is an evangel or good news to receive, not a code to keep. It invites the response of faith from beginning to end.

Paul found support for his basic concept of justification by faith in Habakkuk 2:4, "He who through faith is righteous shall live." The King James Version translates the phrase "by faith" with the verb: "The just shall live by faith." The underlying text is not clear, accounting for the difference in emphasis reflected in these translations. In Paul's understanding of the gospel, right standing with God, faith, and life all belong together.

The Sinfulness of Men
1:18 to 3:20

Pagan Lostness (1:18-32)

In the first major division of his letter, Paul charged the entire human race with its sinfulness before God (1:18 to 3:20). All peoples, both Gentiles (1:18-32) and Jews (2:1 to 3:8), were included in his universal indictment (3:9-20). Together they were inexcusable before him.

However, in this chapter we will focus our attention upon Paul's discussion of pagan lostness in Romans 1:18-32. Wherein lay the guilt of the pagan world of his day? It did not have God's revelation in the law of Moses, and so could not have been guilty of transgressing it. It had not heard of God's supreme revelation in Jesus Christ, and so could not have been guilty of rejecting him. One cannot reject a gospel he has not heard. Nor did Paul charge them with guilt because of Adam's sin, as many have done since. For no appeal is made to Adam's transgression throughout this entire section on the guilt of all men before God.

The answer is to be found in God's revelation to the pagan world and their response to it.

God's Revelation (1:18-20)

Through wrath (1:18).—Already Paul had referred to the revelation of God's righteousness in the gospel (1:17). And this disclosure will be discussed at length in the second major division of his letter (3:20 to 8:39). But now Paul pointed to the revelation of God's wrath in his judgment upon sin: "For the wrath of God is revealed from heaven against all ungodliness and wickedness of men who by their wickedness suppress the truth" (1:18). And Romans 1:19 to 3:20 provides a commentary on this verse.

Both of these revelations are parallel and continuous. That is, God's righteousness is being revealed at all times through the preaching of the gospel of salvation (1:17). Also, God's wrath is always being revealed through his abandonment of men to the consequences of their sinful choices (1:18). The former delivers the repentant one *from* sin, and the latter delivers the unrepentant *to* sin. In a real sense God's mercy is at work in both revelations. Through each, God seeks to prompt men to repentance and faith and thus make right their relationship to him. Sometimes men are not ready for the revelation of God's righteousness through *deliverance* until they have experienced the revelation of God's wrath through *degradation.*

This concept of the wrath of God has distressed many. Some Bible students have sought to soften its harshness by claiming that God does not become angry with men. They have insisted that Paul used the term "wrath" in an impersonal way, referring to the progress of evil merely as a natural effect of men's evil choices, and not as the result of a direct act of God.

But this interpretation seems to dilute Paul's sense in the passage. Throughout the Old and New Testaments God reveals himself, as in other ways, through his judgments upon the sinfulness of men. Protesting any sentimentalizing of the biblical conception of God, A. M. Hunter affirms: "Wrath—the strong and continuous reaction of the holy God against evil in every shape and form—a wrath operative now and not only at the Last Judgment, is an essential part of any truly biblical idea of God."[5]

To be sure, we are not to think of God's wrath in terms of our own peevish displays of bad temper. Instead it is God's relentless opposition to all that would distort and destroy his creation. It is his firm stand against all sin and rebellion. God judges as he judges because he loves as he loves. He seeks to dissuade men from their sins by handing them over to the consequences of their sins. When men rebel against God, they experience now the foretaste of God's wrath, the full manifestation of which awaits the final judgment. (See Rom. 2:5,16; 1 Thess. 1:9; 5:1-11; 2 Thess. 1:5-10; 1 Cor. 4:5; 2 Cor. 5:10).

Through nature (1:19-20).—The pagan world had an opportunity to know God through his revelation in nature: "Ever since the creation of the world his invisible nature, namely, his eternal power and deity, has been clearly perceived in the things that have been made" (1:20; compare Ps. 19:1-4; Acts 14:15-17). Not only does this verse affirm God's disclosure of himself in nature, but also it indicates what may be learned about him, namely, his eternal power and deity. And this was enough knowledge of God to place men under the responsibility of acknowledging him and rendering thanks to him.

Three observations need to be made here: (1) God is the revealer, and nature is the medium of his revelation. This is why it is imprecise to say that nature reveals God. Apart from God's revealing, nature cannot make him known. To confuse or identify the Revealer with the medium of his revelation is the essence of idolatry. (2) God's revelation in nature does not guarantee a positive response. That is, men are as capable of rejecting God's revelation in nature as they are of rejecting his supreme revelation in Jesus Christ. To the psalmist the heavens declared the glory of God (Ps. 19:1), but this was the response of a devout man. For some men the only thing that the heavens tell is whether or not tomorrow will be a good day to plant potatoes or to go fishing. (3) God's revelation of himself in nature establishes the minimal ground of every man's responsibility before him. Nobody has ever had less ground than this as a basis for knowing God. Of course, one may have much more, for example, God's revelation through the law and prophets or his full revelation in Jesus Christ. However, man's responsibility before God is based upon his response to the revelation that God has made available to him. Man cannot reject light that he does not have. It is the *fact* of God's revelation, not its *extent,* that is basic to Paul's argument here. And the validity of God's revelation in nature to the pagan world was essential to Paul's indictment of its inexcusability before God (1:20).

Pagan Response (1:21-23,25)

Rebellion (1:21,25,28).—Man may respond to God's revelation in two ways: in faith or by rejection. He has the capacity to say yes or no to

God and make it stick. For unless he is free to say no to God and have it prevail, he cannot really say yes. Alternatives are essential to choice; and choice, whether positive or negative, is essential to being human. Universalism seeks to rescue God's integrity in the final judgment, but it does so by compromising the integrity of both God and man in creation.

Moreover, no can be just as honest an answer to God as yes. It is the answer of rebellion, whereas faith is the response of trust and commitment. But God loves us enough to respect the integrity of our no, even while seeking our yes. So long as we prefer our will to his, he permits us to have our own way.

How had the pagan world responded to God's revelation through nature? Paul indicated their response in several places. He charged that "although they knew God they did not honor him as God or give thanks to him" (v. 21). Also they "exchanged the glory of the immortal God for images resembling mortal man or birds or animals or reptiles" (v. 23). Again, "they exchanged the truth about God for a lie and worshiped and served the creature rather than the Creator" (v. 25). And in spite of all that God had done, "they did not see fit to acknowledge God" (v. 28).

Note that the guilt of the pagans did not derive from an ignorance of God or his demand. Rather their knowledge of God was assumed, and it was the basis upon which their responsibility rested. God had sought to make himself known to them, but they willfully closed their minds to him.

Arrogance (1:21-22).—When man refuses to have God as God, he dooms himself to have less than God as his god. And he himself is the number one candidate for the honor. He prefers to be his own god. The role of deity better fits his self-estimate. The illusion of complete self-determination exhilarates him. Thus Paul stated that the pagans "became futile in their thinking and their senseless minds were darkened. Claiming to be wise, they became fools" (vv. 21-22).

Paul's keen insight into the nature of sinfulness saw man in revolt against his creatureliness. Paul saw man engaged in a desperate effort to wrest the rights of deity out of the hands of God. This is the meaning of Eden and Babel. Man declares himself to be ultimate or supreme, and fills the air with his blather.

The god mask is the phoniest of all the masks that man wears.

Idolatry (1:23,25).—As rebellion was an improper attitude toward God and arrogance an improper attitude toward self, so idolatry reveals an improper attitude toward creation.

Man's refusal to acknowledge God as God makes idolatry inevitable. It leads to a tragic reversal of the primeval order set forth in Genesis 1:26, "Then God said, 'Let us make man in our image, after our likeness; and let them have dominion over the fish of the sea, and over the birds of the air, and over the cattle, and over all the earth, and over every creeping thing that creeps upon the earth.' " God, the Creator, placed man over the lower animal creation. But in his rebellion against God, arrogant man inverted this order. He sought to exchange "the glory of the immortal God for images resembling mortal man or birds or animals or reptiles" (v. 23). He bartered God's truth for a lie and worshiped the creature rather than the Creator (v. 25).

What a tragic distortion! Man who has refused to worship the Creator winds up worshiping forms of animal life. This is sin's ultimate mockery.

God's Judgment (1:24-32)

Men are free to receive or reject God's revelation. However they are not free to do so without consequences. Thus the current boast of an absolute freedom is a shallow illusion. Is it not ironic that the media constantly ascribe the term "liberated" to those pathetic persons who are the most enslaved to their baser appetites? What kind of tyranny is it that finds its broken-down victims filling the air with proud claims of liberty? These self-designated "beautiful people" have to run fast and play a lot of make-believe to keep their eyes off the fast rate of their inward dying. The only freedom any person has at any time is bound directly to the consequences of his choices.

The rejection of God's revelation has dire results. Paul described those results in one of the most dismal passages in the entire Bible. Like the tolling of a bell, the dreadful clause, "God gave them up," recurs three times in verses 24, 26, and 28.

To impurity (1:24-25).—Paul wrote: "Therefore God gave them up in the lusts of their hearts to impurity, to the dishonoring of their bodies among themselves" (v. 24). The following verse explains this immorality as a result of the rejection of God's truth. Men swapped it for a lie. Confronted by that which should have evoked their adoration, they chose to worship and to serve "the creature rather than the Creator" (v. 25). They defied the created order and created the divine in their own image. Thus God abandoned them to the consequences of their own conceits. And with the removal of the divine restraints, men sank into a self-degrading spiral of sensualism.

Often in the ancient world sexual immorality was the hand-maiden of popular religion. Sacramental fornication was a part of the ritual of many fertility cults. Through imitative magic, intercourse with a cult prostitute was supposed to prompt the goddess and her consort to copulate, thereby assuring harvests, herds, and families. Thus it was particularly difficult to establish a Christian concept of a basic morality between the sexes. Idolatry and immorality provided mutual support. (See Gal. 5:19-21.)

To sexual perversion (1:26-27).—Paul continued, "For this reason God gave them up to dishonorable passions. Their women exchanged natural relations for unnatural, and the men likewise gave up natural relations with women and were consumed with passion for one another, men committing shameless acts with men and receiving in their own person the due penalty for their error" (vv. 26-27).

What does this passage teach about homosexuality? Observe the following:

(1) *Homosexuality is an abandonment to "dishonorable passions" (v. 26).* When men chose to worship the creature rather than the Creator (1:25), the difference between God and his creation was obscured. With this confusion *between* the orders of deity and creatureliness, a confusion of the orders *within* creatureliness appeared. Thus men worshiped animals as gods and used other men for women. In such passions men and women alike dishonored themselves.

(2) *Homosexuality is "unnatural" (v. 26).* The woman who has sexual relations with another woman, and the man who has sexual relations with another man act in ways contrary to God's creation. If practiced universally, it would lead to the extinction of the human race in a short time. Genesis 1:27-28 affirms the maleness and femaleness of the human race. It presents men and women as complementary sexual beings, each essential to the other in the reproduction of their kind. Heterosexuality is the only pattern of sexual conduct that fits God's creative order. Thus when men and women take those of like sex as partners, their conduct is contrary to nature. It is unnatural. The homosexual who says, "God made me as I am," is attributing a confusion to God that simply does not exist.

(3) *Homosexuality involves "shameless acts" (v. 27).* The capacity for

shame is an index of moral sensitivity. Heeded, it performs a valuable function in moral guidance. But outraged by repeated violations, the capacity for shame hardens and eventually dies. Then men will do publicly without remorse that which formerly caused them distress. This moral death they call "liberation."

(4) *Homosexuality is sexual perversion, and results in a serious breakdown for those involved (v. 27).* The word translated "error" here is better rendered "perversion" in *The New English Bible* and *The New International Version.* The context favors the stronger term. In Paul's thought homosexuality is more than a mistake; it is a perversion. Phillips enhances this sense by translating, "receiving in their own personalities the consequences of their perversity." Of moral necessity there is personal retribution in accord with the wrong done.

Needless to say, the biblical teaching about homosexuality differs sharply from the views gaining ground in our culture. What the Bible indicts as sexual perversion, many today describe as an alternate lifestyle. Some homosexual organizations press for the legalization of any kind of sexual relationship between consenting adults. Thus the consent of participating individuals is the only guideline invoked, as though society had no stake in the matter. And some homosexuals have even carried their campaigns into the annual sessions of Christian denominations, seeking recognition and confirmation for their views and practices within the household of faith.

None of these efforts to demand legal sanction, social acceptance, and religious respectability for homosexuality is to be taken lightly. They contradict the plain teaching of the Word of God. Leviticus 18:22 warns, "You shall not lie with a male as with a woman; it is an abomination." (See also Gen. 19:4-5; Lev. 20:13; 1 Tim. 1:10; Jude v. 7.)

The gospel offers homosexuals something far more compassionate than a sanction that leaves them as they are. Through faith in Jesus Christ, it offers them the deliverance to become what God wants them to be. (See 1 Cor. 6:9-11.)

To depraved reason (1:28-32).—Because men had not seen fit to acknowledge God, Paul wrote, "God gave them up to a base mind and to improper conduct" (v. 28). In the Greek text of this verse, there is a play on words that is not indicated in most English translations. The rendering that follows seeks to make Paul's pun more obvious, "Even as *they did not see fit* to acknowledge God, God gave them up to an *unfit* mind, to do the things that are improper" (both translation and italics by author).

Paul proceeded to characterize the life-style of the God-rejecting and thus God-rejected Gentiles, "They were filled with all manner of wickedness, evil, covetousness, malice. Full of envy, murder, strife, deceit, malignity, they are gossips, slanderers, haters of God, insolent, haughty, boastful, inventors of evil, disobedient to parents, foolish, faithless, heartless, ruthless" (vv. 29-31). Twenty-one vices which characterized ancient pagan society are listed here. They marked the lives of those whom God had abandoned to the consequences of their wrong choices. Similar lists of vices may be found in 2 Corinthians 12:20-21; Galatians 5:19-21; Ephesians 5:3-5; Colossians 3:5,8-9; 1 Timothy 1:9-10; 2 Timothy 3:2-5.

These ancient wrongs have a modern ring to them. They seem to describe our world today. Men cannot reject God and build a society in which these destructive qualities do not predominate. And the fact that they cannot constitutes the continuing revelation of God's wrath. The revelation of God's wrath is as authentic as his revelation of righteousness. Every utopia ventured by God-rejecting men is doomed to crumble under the sheer weight of its moral corruption. Abandoned by God, every such undertaking is destined to self-destruct.

The final effect of man's rejection of God is scored in the last verse of the chapter, "Though they know God's decree that those who do such things deserve to die, they not only do them but approve those who practice them" (v. 32). Man's sin is not due to his ignorance of God. Rather man's sin expresses itself in his willful rebellion against God and his tenacious commitment to evil. He knows the justice of God that decrees death for those who practice those things; yet he will not turn from his sins. Conceivably, though choosing this destiny for himself, some vestige of decency or compassion might cause him to desire something better for others. But no! He not only sells out to depravity himself but also applauds a like degeneracy in others.

Is it not remarkable that so much of what the Bible calls reprobation, modern man calls either an illness or an alternate life-style?

Jewish Lostness (2:1 to 3:20)

Pagan lostness as described in Romans 1:18-32 is highly visible. The twenty-one vices Paul cited in verses 29-31 spell out in letters large enough for all to see the depravity of pagan society. They provide one of the most dismal portrayals ever penned of the downward potential of human nature. Here is the pagan life-style of any age or culture, whether first-century Graeco-Roman or twentieth-century American. It is the lostness of a blatant defiance toward God, unrestrained by any fear of consequences.

The climax of pagan degradation is described in Romans 1:32. Here Paul denounced the perversity that lies at the heart of all rebellion against God. The problem did not derive from a lack of opportunity to know God or his will. But in the full knowledge that those committed to such vices deserved death, the pagans reveled in them. Furthermore they approved the same depravity in others. This marked the death of the capacity for shame, which reprobates of every age boldly proclaim as enlightenment. Actually their condition is the outworking of the wrath of God against all ungodliness and wickedness of men (1:18).

But not all rebellion against God takes the form of pagan debauchery. This is why those who equate all lostness with degradation may conclude too quickly that they are rightly related to God. There is a form of lostness that has a religious appearance. It does not look like rebellion against God, because of its concern with religious matters. And yet one may retain an unrepentant heart toward God close to the altar.

Paul described this form of lostness in Romans 2:1 to 3:20, where he turned his attention from the pagan world to his own Jewish people. Notice the features of Jewish lostness that made its rebellion against God difficult to recognize.

Approval of God's Judgment upon Pagan Wrong (2:1-16)

First, the Jews approved of God's judgment upon the pagan world. Unlike the Gentiles described in Romans 1:32, they did not applaud those who practiced pagan vices. Quite to the contrary, they condemned them. In doing so, they revealed a knowledge of God, an awareness of sin, and an acknowledgment of his right to judge it.

Did not the approval of God's judgment upon pagan wrong prove that the Jews were rightly related to God? It should have. But what if those who approved God's judgment upon others were themselves guilty of the same sins? Were they to suppose that they would escape the judgment of God?

Agreement without obedience (2:1-11).—No! Paul charged that by passing judgment upon the Gentiles, the Jews condemned themselves, because they were doing the same things (v. 1). To expect God to condone in themselves the sins he punished in others was to invite God's judgment (v. 3). It was to treat with contempt the great kindness, forbearance, and patience of God (v. 4). These three terms describe a revelation of God that went beyond the disclosure to the Gentiles through nature of his eternal power and deity (1:20). They suggest the divine qualities shown through centuries of God's gracious dealings with the Jews.

God had intended his kindness to the Jews to lead them to repentance (v. 4). Instead they had responded with presumption upon his mercy, assuming a privileged status with regard to divine judgment. While claiming to glory in God's kindness toward them, the Jews actually treated it with contempt. For all praise of God's kindness that does not involve repentance and obedient trust is a despising of it. Such empty praise is the issue of hearts that are hard and impenitent toward God, no matter how expert in the denunciation of the sins of others. Thereby the Jews were storing up wrath for themselves "on the day of wrath when God's righteous judgment will be revealed" (v. 5).

Paul reminded his fellow Jews of God's evenhanded judgment: "He will render to every man according to his works: to those who by patience in well-doing seek for glory and honor and immortality, he will give eternal life; but for those who are factious and do not obey the truth, but obey wickedness, there will be wrath and fury" (vv. 6-8). Rephrasing this principle in verses 9-10, Paul asserted the priority of the Jews to the Gentiles in judgment as well as in salvation (1:16). God's fuller revelation to them established the ground for their greater accountability to him.

Judgment with or without the law (2:12-16).—With respect to the judgment of God, what did having the law mean for the Jews? What did the lack of access to the law of Moses mean for the Gentiles? Could the Jews expect preferential treatment for having it? Or could the Gentiles plead special consideration for not having it? To such concerns Paul next gave his attention.

First, observe what having the law meant for the Jews. To be sure, God's revelation through the law provided a great advantage. (See Rom. 3:1-2.) It made known the will of God more completely, making possible a fuller knowledge of him. But the greater opportunity for knowing the will of God included also a greater responsibility for keeping it. The benefit of the law did not derive from standing in the historical tradition in which it was given. Nor was it in being exposed to hearing the law read in the synagogue services each sabbath. These were potential advantages. But Paul insisted that no benefit accrued to the Jews for hearing the law apart from obedience to it: "It is not the hearers of the law who are righteous before God, but the doers of the law who will be justified" (v. 13). Otherwise, "all who have sinned under the law will be judged by the law" (v. 12).

But what about the Gentiles, who had no access to the fuller revelation of God made available to the Jews through the law of Moses? Would they be able to plead immunity in the judgment? No! Paul wrote, "All who have sinned without the law will also perish without the law" (v. 12). No Gentile would be held responsible for light he did not have. But by the same token he would be judged upon the basis of the revelation that God had made available to him (1:20).

Moreover, there was a real sense in which the Gentiles also had access to the law of God—not the written law, to be sure, but the inner law of conscience. Paul stated, "When Gentiles who have not the law do by nature what the law requires, they are a law to themselves, even though they do not have the law. They show that what the law requires is written on their hearts, while their conscience also bears witness and their conflicting thoughts accuse or perhaps excuse them" (vv. 14-15).

Through the medium of conscience God inscribed what the law required on the hearts of the Gentiles. He affirmed the distinction between right and wrong and demanded that right be chosen and wrong condemned. Thus conscience, as well as nature (1:20), constituted a medium through which God sought to reveal himself to the pagan world. In this way Paul brought all men, Gentiles as well as Jews, under the law of God. Through the law of Moses, God revealed himself to the Jews, and through the law written on the heart, he revealed himself to the Gentiles. And according to the gospel Paul preached, God would judge the secrets of both Jews and Gentiles by Christ Jesus on the last day (v. 16).

Readiness to Instruct Pagans in God's Ways (2:17-24)

A second feature of Jewish lostness that made its rebellion against God difficult to recognize was its missionary zeal. Did not the knowledge of God's will and the eagerness to share it with pagans prove that the Jews were rightly related to God? It should have. But what if those who readily proclaimed the will of God to others were themselves indifferent to its demands? Does God exempt from the keeping of his will those who proclaim it?

Advantages of the Jews (2:17-20).—In the original text, verses 17-20 constitute one long conditional sentence. Paul emphasized real, rather than merely potential, action. That is, the attitudes and conduct attributed to the Jew in these four verses were not hypothetical or imaginary. They were actual, and they added up to a lofty self-estimate.

Observe the details Paul mentioned in his elaboration of the advantages of the Jews and their pride regarding them.

(1) *You call yourself a Jew (v. 17).* The earliest use of the name "Jew" in the Old Testament is found in 2 Kings 16:6. (The RSV renders the plural noun of the Hebrew text, "The men of Judah.") Both during and following the Exile the name gained currency. The Jew was proud to be known as a Jew.

(2) *You rely upon the law (v. 17).* The verb translated "rely upon" occurs only twice in the New Testament: Luke 10:6 and here. The sense is that of finding rest or support in something. Thus the Jew leaned upon or found support in the law.

(3) *You glory in God (v. 17).* No man has a higher privilege or capacity than this: to have his boast or glory in God. This is the heart of worship. (See Isa. 45:25; Jer. 9:24; 1 Cor. 1:31.)

(4) *You know his will (v. 18).* The original text reads simply "the will." Yet the context and common usage make plain that God's will is intended. The law was regarded as the full revelation of the will of God.

(5) *You approve what is excellent (v. 18).* The phrase translated "what is excellent" could mean "the things that differ." Thus *The New English Bible* renders, "You know right from wrong." In either instance Paul stated that the reason the Jews had this capacity was that they were instructed in the law.

(6) *You are sure that you are a guide to the blind, a light to those in darkness, a corrector of the foolish, a teacher of children (vv. 19-20).* All the terms applied to the Jew—"guide," "light," "corrector," "teacher"—are self-praising. And all the terms applied to the Gentiles—"blind," "darkness," "foolish," "children" express a low opinion. They reveal both the high esteem in which the Jew held himself and the low regard that he had for the Gentiles.

Inconsistencies of the Jews (2:21-24).—Paul used a roll call of Jewish boasts to set up his fellow Jews for the censure found in verses 21-24. The charge took the form of five rhetorical questions (vv. 21-23) and a pronouncement (v. 24). Observe that in each of the questions Paul charged the Jews with a shocking gap between their profession and their practice. Thus these verses serve to detail the charge made against the Jews in Romans 2:3.

(1) *You who teach another, do you not teach yourself (v. 21)?* One has to know the truth to teach it. Will one venture to teach to others what he does not apply to himself?

(2) *You who preach against stealing, do you steal (v. 21)?* This is the Eighth Commandment. There are many forms of robbery. The prophet Amos denounced the greedy merchants who were eager for religious holidays to pass so that they could resume their sale of wheat with dishonest balances (Amos 8:5).

(3) *You who say not to commit adultery, do you commit adultery (v. 22)?* This is the Seventh Commandment. One calls to mind here the incident of the woman taken in the act of adultery and brought before Jesus, as recorded in some ancient texts of John 7:53 to 8:11.

(4) *You who detest idols, do you rob temples (v. 22)?* The verb translated "do you rob temples" only occurs here in the New Testament. The adjective form of this word occurs only in Acts 19:37, where the Revised Standard Version renders it "sacrilegious." These two translations indicate the dispute over the meaning of the word: either to rob temples or, more generally, to commit some irreverent act against a holy place.

(5) *You who glory in the law, do you dishonor God by transgressing the law (v. 23)?* Transgressing the law made the Jews' boast in it an empty gesture. God wanted no praise of his revelation in the law at the expense of obedience to it. Moreover, disobedience to God's revelation in the law made the Jews the priest-nation in reverse! Instead of leading Gentiles to seek and praise God by their faithfulness, they caused them to blaspheme his name by their transgressions. Paul cited Isaiah 52:5 in support of his charge.

In the same way Christians today can cause others to scorn God by their shoddy discipleship.

Obedience to the Requirement of Circumcision (2:25-29)

A third feature of Jewish lostness that obscured its alienation from God was its faithful observance of the law requiring circumcision. Though this rite was practiced by other peoples in the ancient world, it had a special meaning for the Jews. God had commanded Abraham, "This is my covenant, which you shall keep, between me and you and your descendants after you: Every male among you shall be circumcised. You shall be circumcised in the flesh of your foreskins, and it shall be a sign of the covenant between me and you" (Gen. 17:10-11). Nor was this command to be taken lightly, for God had warned, "Any uncircumcised male who is not circumcised in the flesh of his foreskin shall be cut off from his people; he has broken my covenant" (Gen. 17:14). No wonder the Jews attached great significance to circumcision.

Did not obedience to the requirement of circumcision prove that the Jew was in a covenant relationship with God? It should have. But what if a circumcised Jew broke the law? Did the rite itself guarantee the relationship it signified?

When circumcision becomes uncircumcision (2:25-27).—No! Paul acknowledged the value of circumcision but insisted upon the obedience to the law that the rite signified: "Circumcision indeed is of value if you obey the law; but if you break the law, your circumcision becomes uncircumcision" (v. 25).

In verse 26 Paul applied this insight to the Gentiles. If a Jew's disobedience to the law made his circumcision an uncircumcision, would not a Gentile's obedience to the law render his uncircumcision a circumcision?

And in the following verse Paul carried this line of reasoning still further, "Then those who are physically uncircumcised but keep the law will condemn you who have the written code and circumcision but break the law" (v. 27). Here Paul placed the uncircumcised Gentiles, who kept the precepts of the law without having it, above the circumcised Jews, who had the law but did not keep it. (See Matt. 12:41-42, where Jesus pronounced a similar judgment upon the Jews.)

The real Jew and true circumcision (2:28-29).—This logic led Paul to conclude what it meant to be a Jew and what constituted circumcision. Verse 28 presents the negative side of the argument, "He is not a real Jew who is one outwardly, nor is true circumcision something external and physical." Verse 29 presents the positive affirmation, "He is a Jew who is one inwardly, and real circumcision is a matter of the heart, spiritual and not literal." (See Gal. 5:6; 6:15; 1 Cor. 7:19; Col. 2:11.)

The words translated "spiritual and not literal" in the Revised Standard Version are rendered more adequately in the following versions: "directed not by written precepts but by the Spirit" (NEB); "this is the work of God's Spirit, not of the written Law" (TEV); "by the Spirit, not by the written code" (NIV). All these find here a reference to the Spirit of God rather than to the spirit of man.

In the last part of verse 29 Paul referred to the original meaning of the term "Jew," namely, "praise." (See Gen. 29:35; 49:8.) Thus the real Jew is one "whose praise is not from men but from God."

Responses to an Imaginary Jewish Objector (3:1-8)

At this point Paul stopped to defend his indictment of Jewish lostness against the objections of an imaginary opponent. No doubt, he had actually encountered such questions from Jewish hearers during his missionary preaching.

What advantage has the Jew? (3:1-2).—What Paul had just written about true Jewish identity and real circumcision was shocking to his fellow Jews (2:25-29). No wonder then that Jewish hearers had likely asked him in many disputes, "Then what advantage has the Jew? Or what is the value of circumcision?" (v. 1).

Paul's answer to his self-imposed question was, "Much in every way. To begin with, the Jews are entrusted with the oracles of God" (v. 2). This sounds as though Paul were going to cite several Jewish advantages. Actually, he did not get past the first one, though later in Romans 9:1-5 he listed others.

Some interpreters identify these oracles with the Ten Commandments. Others associate them with the messianic promises of the Old Testament. Most likely the reference is to the whole Old Testament.

Does Jewish unfaithfulness nullify God's faithfulness? (3:3-4).—In the previous chapter Paul had spoken of those hardened and impenitent Jews who were storing up wrath for themselves (2:5). He had described those who were proclaiming the law fervently to the Gentiles but were practicing it shoddily before them (2:21-24). Obviously they were being faithless with regard to the covenant. Now then, the unfaithfulness of some Jews did not nullify the faithfulness of God, did it?

Paul's response was emphatic, "By no means! Let God be true though every man be false" (v. 4). And he supported his words with a quote from the last part of Psalm 51:4. The point of the reference to this great penitential psalm is God's vindication in judgment.

Is not God unjust to impose his wrath upon us? (3:5-6).—The imaginary Jewish objector now began to question God's justice. He argued that his wickedness actually served God by providing a contrasting background for God's righteousness. Thus, would not God be unjust to reward such service with punishment? (v. 5).

What a twisted concept of divine service this represents! Again Paul reacted strongly to his self-imposed question. By the explanation, "I speak in a human way," he apologized for subjecting the righteousness of God to the indignity of such an argument (v. 5). And he repeated the exclamation of revulsion used in verse 4, "By no means! For then how could God judge the world?" (v. 6). The moral governorship of the universe was at stake in such an absurd charge.

Does not my falsehood cause God's truth to abound? (3:7-8).—The contrast in verse 5 was between the wickedness of the Jew and the righteousness of God. Here the contrast is between the falsehood of the Jew and the truth of God. Otherwise the thought is much the same. In one instance, the Jew suggested that his wickedness served to show the righteousness of God to such an advantage that God would be unjust to punish him for it. In the other, he suggested that his falsehood so caused the truth of God to abound to his glory, that he wondered why he was still being condemned as a sinner. What both amounted to was an evangelistic appeal, "Why not do evil that good may come?" (v. 8). Indeed, some had slandered Paul by charging that this was what he preached. Paul retorted, "Their condemnation is just" (v. 8).

God does not need our evil as a *contrast* to his goodness. Rather he wants our goodness as a *reflection* of his likeness. It praises his glory when God is permitted to create his righteousness in us. Surely those who rationalize their wickedness as a way of achieving God's glory are more evil than those who openly defy God in their depravity (1:32). This is why the impenitence of the religious man is more treacherous than pagan revolt. None is so hardened against God as those who have maintained their rebellion against him close to the altar. (See Jesus' condemnation of Jewish religious leaders in Matt. 21:31-32.)

Conclusion: All Are Guilty Before God (3:9-20)

No fear of God before their eyes (3:9-18).—The translation of Romans 3:9 remains uncertain. The problem centers in the meaning of the verb rendered, "Are we . . . any better off?" The same form is capable of the meaning, "Are we . . . at any disadvantage?" (See RSV margin.) Thus we cannot be sure whether Paul asked about a supposed Jewish advantage or disadvantage, though the former seems more likely.

However, no uncertainty exists about his charge that all men, both Gentiles (1:18-32) and Jews (2:1 to 3:8) are under the power of sin (v.

9). To support his charge, Paul strung together several Old Testament passages, much after the rabbinical pattern (vv. 10-18). His selections were made from Psalm 14:1-3 (vv. 10-12); Psalm 5:9; 140:3 (v. 13); Psalm 10:7 (v. 14); Isaiah 59:7-8 (vv. 15-17); and Psalm 36:1 (v. 18). Together they led up to the ultimate condemnation of verse 18, "There is no fear of God before their eyes." This verse states the *cause* for all of the disastrous *effects* listed in verses 10-17, which were so visible in Paul's day—and our own.

The whole world is accountable to God (3:19-20).—In bringing his indictment of all men to a close, Paul wrote, "Now we know that whatever the law says it speaks to those who are under the law, so that every mouth may be stopped, and the whole world may be held accountable to God" (3:19). Those under the law are Jews. Paul focused attention upon them, that they might understand that they, as well as the Gentiles, were answerable to God. Both were without excuse before him (1:20; 2:1).

Quoting rather freely from Psalm 143:2 Paul added, "No human being will be justified in his sight by works of the law, since through the law comes the knowledge of sin" (3:20). At one time Paul had believed that righteousness was to be achieved through keeping the law. (See Phil. 3:6,9.) Then he learned that the law did not make possible a right standing with God. But it did perform the useful function of creating a consciousness of sin. This important concept will be treated at greater length in Romans 7:7-25.

The Grace of God

3:21 to 8:39

The Heart of the Gospel (3:21 to 4:25)

Romans 3:21 begins with "But now," and we may be grateful for these two words. They mark a turning point in Paul's discussion. Having exposed the sinfulness of men in Romans 1:18 to 3:20, Paul now turned to declare the grace of God in Romans 3:21 to 8:39. As the former passage depicted man's bondage *to* sin, so the latter proclaimed his deliverance *from* sin. Thus at this point Paul returned to the theme of his letter introduced in Romans 1:16-17, namely, the revelation of the righteousness of God.

The next three chapters of this commentary are devoted to the second major division of the letter, Romans 3:21 to 8:39. No finer presentation of the gospel of God's grace is to be found anywhere in the New Testament.

In the present chapter attention is directed first to Romans 3:21-31. Here Paul set forth the heart of the gospel as he had both experienced and proclaimed it. Then we will move on to Romans 4:1-25, a passage featuring God's dealings with Abraham. Paul presented him as the foremost example in the Old Testament of justification by faith.

God's Way of Making Us Right with Himself (3:21-31)

Apart from law (3:21).—As a devout Pharisee, Paul had believed that he could achieve a right standing with God through keeping the law. Thus he was extremely zealous for the traditions of the fathers (Gal. 1:14). He claimed that he was blameless with regard to righteousness under the law (Phil. 3:6). However, his encounter with the risen Christ on the road to Damascus radically changed all this. No longer did Paul depend upon his obedience to the law as the basis for his acceptance with God. Rather those features of Jewish heritage and boasting that had formerly been his "gain," he now counted "as loss" (Phil. 3:7). Gladly he forfeited them for Christ's sake. Thus he declared, "For his sake I have suffered the loss of all things, and count them as refuse, in order that I may gain Christ and be found in him, not having a righteousness of my own, based on law, but that which is through faith in Christ, the righteousness from God that depends on faith" (Phil. 3:8-9).

When God confronts us in the gospel of Jesus Christ, he does not lay down a new law for us to keep. We are not invited to attain a right standing with him through obedience to any religious code. Paul wrote, "But now the righteousness of God has been manifested *apart from law*" (v. 21). The gospel is nonlegalistic. It is an evangel, God's good news to a sinful race.

Attested by the Law and the Prophets (3:21).—In Romans 1:2 Paul indicated that God had promised the gospel beforehand through his prophets in the Holy Scriptures. Here he expanded the statement to include the Law as well as the Prophets. Through both, God had borne witness to his saving acts in Jesus Christ. The gospel was no innovation.

Thus Paul shared with other early Christians the conviction that the Old Testament pointed forward to the coming of Jesus Christ. (See Luke 24:44-47; 1 Pet. 1:10-11.) The great promises of the Old Testament have their fulfillment in the New.

Experienced through faith in Jesus Christ (3:22-25).—Paul affirmed that God made available to men a right relationship to himself through faith in Jesus Christ (v. 22). All men need to believe in him, "since all have sinned and fall short of the glory of God" (v. 23). This latter clause is the verdict Paul reached regarding the Gentiles (1:18-32) and the Jews (2:1 to 3:20), and he repeated it here.

Scholars differ in their understanding of the reference to "the glory of God" in verse 23. Note the following proposals: (1) Some relate it to the rabbinic idea of the *divine splendor* that Adam lost in the fall. At the end time, when God made the new world, man would regain this lost glory. But Paul taught that man regained it when he was justified. (2) Some claim that Paul spoke of the glory of God as a future goal that man in his sin has not yet reached (2:10; 5:2; 6:4; 8:18; 1 Cor. 15:43; 2 Cor. 3:18). (3) Still others regard the glory of God as the divine likeness that God intends man to bear now. Insofar as man falls short of this divine likeness, he is sinful.

Verses 24-25 are crucial for our understanding of Paul's teaching regarding the death of Jesus Christ on the cross. Unfortunately, they are difficult to translate. Also they use metaphors whose meanings require careful study. Paul wrote, "They are justified by his grace as a gift, through the redemption which is in Christ Jesus, whom God put forward as an expiation by his blood, to be received by faith" (vv. 24-25).

Observe the three metaphors Paul used here to describe what God has done for sinful men through Jesus Christ, his Son.

(1) *The metaphor of the courtroom (v. 24).* The important word here is translated "they are justified." The active form of the verb means "to justify," "to pronounce righteous," "to put in the right," or "to acquit." It is a legal term used by courts.

The picture here depicts sinful man as guilty before the bar of a righteous judge. He stands awaiting the dreadful sentence that he merits because of his sins. However, because of that which Jesus Christ accomplished on the cross, the guilty man hears the verdict, "Acquitted!"

Historically there has been much debate between the so-called forensic and vital views of justification. The former stresses the paradox and affirms, "God acquits the guilty!" The latter rightly insists that God does not simply declare a guilty man to be innocent. Instead God creates his righteousness in the one whom he acquits. He puts him in the right.

(2) *The metaphor of slavery (v. 24).* The important word here is translated "redemption." The word was used in the ancient world to describe the liberation of slaves or prisoners of war. Often this involved the payment of a sum of money or a ransom.

The term also has a rich background in the Old Testament. It was used to describe God's deliverance of Israel from bondage in Egypt. Why did God do this? Deuteronomy 7:8 explains, "It is because the Lord loves you, and is keeping the oath which he swore to your fathers, that the Lord has brought you out with a mighty hand, and *redeemed* you from the house of bondage, from the hand of Pharaoh king of Egypt" (author's italics). Later during the Babylonian Exile the prophet assured the people that "the *ransomed* of the Lord shall return, and come to Zion with singing" (Isa. 51:11, author's italics).

When this slave metaphor is applied to the meaning of the cross, sinful man is portrayed as enslaved man. God is the benefactor who redeems him from bondage. He does this through the death of Jesus Christ, his Son, as a redemptive act. Through faith in Christ enslaved man is set free.

(3) *The metaphor of ritual sacrifice (v. 25).* The important word here is translated "expiation." This form occurs only two times in the New Testament: verse 25 and Hebrews 9:5. In the latter passage it is translated "mercy seat," and some scholars argue that it carries the same sense here. (See Lev. 16:1-34 for the background of this concept in the annual observance of the Day of Atonement.)

However, none of the standard translations renders the word as "mercy seat" in verse 25. Instead, for example, the King James Version translates it "propitiation." Among pagan writers of the ancient world the word usually meant "to appease" or "to placate." When applied to a god, it carried the idea of the appeasement of an angry deity by an offering. Some sacrifice was made, in order to turn aside the wrath of an offended or vengeful god.

Conceived in this way, the death of Christ on the cross was a sacrificial act that averted the wrath of God from sinners. By placing their faith in Christ, men escaped God's anger.

As indicated above, the Revised Standard Version translates the word

in question "expiation." How much better is "expiation" than "propitiation" as a translation? For the average reader of the Bible, the translation is little, if any better, since he uses neither word in his daily conver-
sation. But for the careful student there is a significant difference.
"Propitiation" means the performance of a sacrificial act to appease an
angry God. The wrath of God is turned aside or placated. "Expiation,"
on the other hand, means the performance of a sacrificial act to annul
the guilt of a sinful man. The guilt or defilement of man is forgiven or
removed.

Regarded as an expiation, Christ's death on the cross was a sacrificial
act through which man's guilt was forgiven. The barrier of guilt standing in the way of God's forgiveness was taken away.

A summary statement regarding Paul's use of these three metaphors
may now be ventured. What is it that God has done for sinful man
through the death of Jesus Christ on the cross? Through the legal metaphor we see a condemned man in a courtroom who hears the verdict of
acquittal. Through the slave metaphor we see an enslaved man who is
redeemed from his bondage and set free. Through the sacrificial metaphor we see a guilty man from whom the wrath of God has been
averted (propitiation). Or we see a man whose guilt has been removed
and sins forgiven (expiation). However conceived, it is all of grace. And
what God has accomplished through the death of his Son on the cross
may be experienced by men through faith.

Shows the righteousness of God (3:25-26).—Why was the death of
Christ on the cross necessary for the demonstration of God's righteousness? Paul explained: "This was to show God's righteousness, because in
his divine forbearance he had passed over former sins" (v. 25).

This does not mean that God had failed to judge the sins of men in
the ancient world. Indeed Romans 1:18 describes the continuous revelation of God's wrath against all ungodliness and wickedness. But it does
look back over the times in which men did not receive the full measure
of judgment for their sins. Why did God withhold the full expression of
his wrath? Paul attributed this restraint to God's forbearance. This was
the same divine quality he had mentioned in Romans 2:4. Along with
God's kindness and patience, it was supposed to lead men to repentance.

Yet when God passed over the sins of the wicked, it raised questions
about his own righteousness. Can God be just and fail to mete out to the
ungodly the judgment they deserve? Does his reluctance to punish indi-

cate an indifference to sin? Paul's answer was to point men to the cross.
No one can stand at the foot of the cross where Jesus died and charge
God with indifference to sin. God abhors sin and judges it. But his judg-
ment falls upon Jesus Christ his Son, who died in our behalf.

What a tragedy when men misinterpret the forbearance or mercy of
God as his indifference toward their sins! (See Eccl. 8:11.)

A further question remains: What was God's purpose in the manifestation of his righteousness through the death of Christ on the cross? Paul
continued, "It was to prove at the present time that he himself is
righteous and that he justifies him who has faith in Jesus" (v. 26).

For God to have been just only would have been relatively simple. All
that was necessary was the speedy execution of his judgment upon sinful
men. But bare, unrelieved justice does not commend itself to God. Not
only would God show himself just but also he seeks to justify sinful men.
This vastly complicates the matter. Only God's infinite resources of
grace could achieve so large a task. And he does it by way of the cross of
Jesus Christ.

Excludes pride (3:27-28).—What implications does justification by
faith have for us at the point of our basic attitude toward God and ourselves? Needless to say, it should make a difference. Those who
imagine that they have attained a right standing with God by keeping
the law tend to be proud. But when God's grace is rightly understood,
pride becomes an early casualty. Paul said, "It is excluded" (v. 27). It is
not that the religious legalist boasts, and the child of God's grace does
not. Both boast. But whereas the legalist boasts in himself (Luke
18:11-12), the Christian boasts in the Lord (Gal. 6:14). Experiencing
God's grace shifts the center of boasting from self to the Savior. Paul
warned the Corinthians, "Let him who boasts, boast of the Lord" (1
Cor. 1:31; literally "in the Lord").

Affirms God as the God of all men (3:29-30).—Another important
implication of justification by faith is that it affirms the universality of
God. That is, since God is one, he is the God of all men, Gentiles as well
as Jews. This belief was stated by devout Jews every time they recited
their traditional confession of faith (the *Shema*), "Hear, O Israel: The
Lord our God is one Lord; and you shall love the Lord your God with
all your heart, and with all your soul, and with all your might" (Deut.
6:4).

Furthermore, the one God has but one way of putting men right with
himself: "He will justify the circumcised on the ground of their faith

and the uncircumcised through their faith" (v. 30).

Upholds the law (3:31).—Does justification by faith destroy the law? No doubt some of Paul's Jewish hearers concluded that it did and raised this objection to his preaching. But Paul was repulsed by such a charge and replied, "By no means! On the contrary, we uphold the law" (v. 31).

In what way did the preaching of justification by faith uphold the law? How did it put the law in proper perspective? Certainly it destroyed the hope of those who were depending upon a righteousness based on the law. But then, God had never intended the law to be the means whereby men attained a right standing with him. This lay beyond its power. (See Gal. 3:21.) The law's function was more modest, as Paul indicated in Romans 3:20, "No human being will be justified in his sight by works of the law, since through the law comes knowledge of sin." (See 4:15; 5:13; 7:7-25; and especially Gal. 3:19 to 4:7.)

To refute those who impose a false function upon the law is to spare it a harmful distortion. Then it is possible to present the law in its true function as an instrument through which God reveals to men their sinfulness. In this sense the preaching of justification by faith upholds the law. It indicates the role God intended for the law in his plan of redemption.

Abraham: Old Testament Example of Justification by Faith (4:1-25)

Will any Jew claim that he needs no justification by faith because he is descended from Abraham? (See Matt. 3:7-10.) Then let him take a closer look at the Scriptures, whose authority he acknowledges. There he will discover that Abraham himself was the foremost Old Testament example (or prototype) of justification by faith.

The basis of Abraham's righteousness (4:1-8).—What was the ground of Abraham's righteousness before God: faith or works? The answer given in Jewish tradition was works. For example, Sirach 44:19-20 (an apocryphal work dated early in the second century BC) stated, "Abraham was the father of a multitude of nations,/and no one has been found like him in glory;/he kept the law of the Most High,/and was taken into covenant with him."[6]

One might well wonder how Abraham managed to keep the law since it was not given until the time of Moses. (See Ex. 19:16 to 24:18.) According to some Jewish tradition Abraham kept the law by anticipation.

It follows then that if Abraham were justified by works (or faith regarded as a work of merit), he had ground for boasting (4:2). However, Paul appealed to Genesis 15:6 to show that this was not so: "What does the scripture say? 'Abraham believed God, and it was reckoned to him as righteousness' " (v. 3). This was a basic biblical teaching about Abraham. God had revealed himself to Abraham, and Abraham had responded in faith. This faith was reckoned to him as righteousness. He was justified by faith.

Work and wages belong together, even as faith and gift do. So if a man works and receives money, the money is not regarded as a gift (v. 4). Instead it is payment for services rendered. On the other hand, if a man receives money that he has not worked for, the money is a gift. With Abraham in mind, Paul applied his metaphor, "To one who does not work but trusts him who justifies the ungodly, his faith is reckoned as righteousness" (v. 5). And David was cited in support of this principle, because he pronounced "a blessing upon the man to whom God reckons righteousness apart from works" (v. 6). The quotation in verses 7-8 is from Psalm 32:1-2.

The meaning of circumcision (4:9-12).—What about this blessing of a righteousness that is reckoned through faith? Is it for the circumcised only or does it also include the uncircumcised?

Once again Paul appealed to what the Scriptures taught about Abraham. He asked his readers to recall whether Abraham's righteousness had been reckoned to him *before* or *after* he was circumcised (v. 10). Of course it was before. The account of his justification by faith is recorded in Genesis 15:6, and his circumcision is not described until Genesis 17:22-27. This was several years later, when Ishmael was thirteen years old (Gen. 17:25). Thus at the time that Abraham's faith was reckoned to him for righteousness, he was as uncircumcised as any Gentile.

Then what was the meaning of circumcision for Abraham? Paul explained, "He received circumcision as a sign or seal of the righteousness which he had by faith while he was still uncircumcised" (v. 11). Circumcision was not the work by means of which Abraham attained a right relationship with God. Rather it was a sign of the justifying faith he already had while uncircumcised. Circumcision was a sign of faith, not a substitute for it.

This had important meaning for Jews and Gentiles alike. Paul asserted, "The purpose was to make him the father of all who believe without being circumcised and who thus have righteousness reckoned to them, and likewise the father of the circumcised who are not merely circumcised but also follow the example of the faith which our father Abraham had before he was circumcised" (4:11-12). Abrahamic sonship is more a matter of likeness of faith than a similarity of bloodlines or traditional rites.

The promise of many descendants (4:13-25).—What of God's promise to Abraham and his descendants that they would inherit the world? Did this come through the law or through the righteousness of faith (v. 13)? It was through faith. Legalism in religion is contrary to faith and promise. It empties faith of its meaning and destroys promise (v. 14). Moreover, the law produces wrath. It lays down God's standard and thus makes transgression possible (v. 15).

Actually faith is the only response on man's part that is compatible with God's grace. The promise rests upon the grace of God and is received through faith (v. 16). The promise is guaranteed to all Abraham's descendants, Gentiles as well as Jews (vv. 16-17). The authority and power of God stand behind it. And he is the one "who gives life to the dead and calls into existence the things that do not exist" (v. 17).

Against the background of this description of God's great power, Paul described faith at work in the life of Abraham (vv. 18-22). God had promised him that he would become the father of many nations (v. 18). Yet at the time the promise was made, circumstances prevailed that made its fulfillment seem impossible. For one thing, Abraham was about one hundred years old (v. 19). Too much should not be made of this, however, since at an even later time Abraham fathered several children by Keturah (Gen. 25:1-2). Of much greater consequence was the fact of Sarah's sterility (v. 19). During normal childbearing years she had been unable to conceive and give birth to a child. Now she was old.

Under circumstances as adverse as these, Abraham demonstrated his faith in God. He was aware, as intelligent faith always is, of every human factor that stood in the way of God's promise. But what did he do? Paul wrote, "No distrust made him waver concerning the promise of God, but he grew strong in his faith as he gave glory to God, fully convinced that God was able to do what he had promised. That is why his faith was 'reckoned to him as righteousness' " (vv. 20-22).

Paul climaxed his account of Abraham's justification by faith by reminding his readers that it had meaning for them, too (vv. 23-25). For the faith of those "who believe in him that raised from the dead Jesus our Lord" (v. 24) is also reckoned as righteousness. Moreover, Jesus "was put to death for our trespasses and raised for our justification" (v. 25).

Made Right with God (5:1 to 6:23)

Now Paul turned his attention to some of the marvelous consequences of justification. In Romans 5:1-11 he described certain benefits it assured. In Romans 5:12-21 he magnified the new humanity headed by Jesus Christ. And in Romans 6:1-23 he declared the power of the gospel of God's grace to change men's lives.

The Benefits of Justification (5:1-11)

Three times in Romans 5:1-11 Paul used forms of the verb translated "rejoice." "We rejoice in our hope of sharing the glory of God" (v. 2); "we rejoice in our sufferings" (v. 3); and "we also rejoice in God through our Lord Jesus Christ" (v. 11). With the exception of James (1:9; 4:16), Paul was the only New Testament writer to use this word. It appears in his letters about thirty-five times. In fact, the recurrence of this word in the present passage sets forth its tone of praise and exultation.

A new relationship to God (5:1-2).—Three words in verses 1-2 characterize the new relationship to God that faith in Jesus Christ makes possible. They are peace, access, and hope. We will look at each one in turn.

First, faith in Jesus Christ makes possible a relationship to God, in which *peace* is established (v. 1). Before men are justified by faith, they are at enmity with God. Their hostility may be expressed in flagrant defiance, as in the case of the pagans described in Romans 1:32. Or it may take the form of impenitence in the midst of religious practices, as in the case of the Jews described in Romans 2:1 to 3:20. Both are forms of rebellion against God, and each abides under his wrath (1:18; 2:5).

But justification by faith changes all this. In the place of the old enmity, now peace reigns between man and God. Man's pretensions have been laid aside. Distrust gives way to glad submission. Arrogance yields to a grateful acceptance of God's gracious way of making sinful men right with himself.

This concept involves more than an inward feeling of peace of mind.

Rather man's status before God has been changed from enmity to peace. Feelings of peace derive from this changed status; they do not determine it.

Immature Christians sometimes tend to be tossed between emotional highs and lows. They need to realize that their feelings at any given time have no effect upon the death that Jesus Christ has already died for their sins. Our salvation does not depend upon our feelings; rather it is based upon his finished work on the cross.

The use of the term "peace" here anticipated the introduction of the metaphor of reconciliation in Romans 5:10-11.

Second, faith in Jesus Christ provides *access* to the grace in which we stand (v. 2). The word translated *access* occurs only three times in the New Testament: Ephesians 2:18; 3:12; and here. In each instance it is applied to Christ. The word denotes an introduction into the presence of an exalted person. Thus Christ is portrayed as the one who ushers us into the sphere of God's grace, in which we stand before God.

Compare this with the limited access of Israel to God, as symbolized in the rites of the Day of Atonement. Of all the hosts of Israel, only the high priest could enter the holy of holies. He could do so only once a year after careful preparations had been made. The people had to wait outside while their priestly representative entered the holy of holies in their behalf. There in God's presence the high priest sprinkled sacrificial blood upon the mercy seat, covering the sins of the people and assuring forgiveness. However, the high priest never did usher the forgiven people into the holy of holies. Instead, after the sacrifices for sins had been made, the people returned to their homes. The curtains closed upon the awesome place of God's special presence for another year.

What a great difference Jesus Christ has made at the point of our access to the sphere of God's grace! We do not stand outside, waiting upon the priestly services of another, who alone has access to the mercy seat. Rather we stand within, as those who have been ushered into the sphere of God's grace through the sacrificial death of Jesus Christ.

Third, faith in Jesus Christ inspires rejoicing in the *hope* of sharing the glory of God (v. 2). Having been justified by faith, we enjoy peace with God in the place of the old enmity (v. 1). And we have been ushered into the sphere of God's grace, in which we stand (v. 2). Thus we can face the future with joy as we hope to share in the glory of God.

Interpreters differ here, as in Romans 3:23, about the meaning of the glory of God. Those who regard it as the divine splendor that Adam lost in the fall anticipate its full recovery at the last day. Those who regard it as the future goal that God intends for man anticipate its fulfillment in the age to come. Those who regard it as God's ideal for man now rejoice in hope, because they know that the goal is attainable. Common to all these views is the hope of sharing the glory of God as the climax of justification by faith.

A new understanding in suffering (5:3-5).—Paul went so far as to write, "We rejoice in our sufferings" (v. 3). Needless to say, this response is not usual in times of trouble. But notice the reason which made Paul so positive, "Knowing that suffering produces endurance, and endurance produces character, and character produces hope" (vv. 3-4).

This process is not fantasy. It is solid recognition that God can turn experiences of suffering into times of spiritual growth and discovery. Observe the sequence that Paul indicated.

First, "suffering produces endurance" (v. 3). The word translated "suffering" literally means "pressure." It describes distress that is brought upon us by outward circumstances.

The noun translated "endurance" is a compound word. It consists of a noun meaning "staying" and a preposition meaning "under." It denotes staying power, the capacity for staying under a heavy burden or load. The concept is not one of passive endurance. Rather it describes the attitude of overcoming. One triumphantly bears and actively overcomes the afflictions that threaten to grind him into the dust. Times of suffering provide opportunity to develop this staying power.

Second, "endurance produces character" (v. 4). The word translated "character" describes the quality of being approved. It was used of metal whose impurities had been purged by fire. Even so the endurance of trial tends to burn the dross out of our lives. It reduces our want list drastically. It makes us men and women of approved or tested character.

Third, "character produces hope" (v. 4). Observe that hope is the final level in these three steps toward spiritual maturity. It always burns most brightly in those whose character has been developed through overcoming many trials. Hope is not the tuition we pay as we enroll in the school of adversity. Rather it is the diploma awarded to those who by the grace of God do well on the tests.

Paul maintained that the Christian's hope "does not disappoint us" (v. 5). It will never prove to be illusory, "because God's love has been poured into our hearts through the Holy Spirit which has been given to us" (v. 5).

A new assurance in judgment (5:6-11).—Another benefit of justification is the assurance it makes possible with regard to the final judgment. Here we learn that Christian hope is neither wishful thinking nor
guesswork. Rather it is based upon the solid foundation of God's love
for us.

In verses 6-8 Paul sought to show the greatness of God's love for sinful
men by comparing it with human love. Regarding man's love he wrote,
"Why, one will hardly die for a righteous man—though perhaps for a
good man one will dare even to die" (v. 7). The distinction Paul intended between the "righteous" man and the "good" man is far from
obvious. However, the point he is making is clear enough. None of us
would find it easy to die for another. And if called upon to do so, it
would help if the one for whom we died were a worthy person.

But what about God's love for us? It was expressed in the death of
Jesus Christ for the unworthy: "While we were yet helpless, at the right
time Christ died for the ungodly" (v. 6). With difficulty a man would
die in behalf of a righteous or good person. But Christ died for sinners.
In one of the greatest verses Paul ever wrote he restated this thought:
"God shows his love for us in that while we were yet sinners Christ died
for us" (v. 8).

The Christian's assurance regarding the final judgment is based upon
what God has already done. Paul stated, "Since, therefore, we are now
justified by his blood, much more shall we be saved by him from the
wrath of God" (v. 9). He repeated this argument and introduced the
metaphor of reconciliation in verse 10.

The wonder that defies all understanding is that God ever reconciled
us to himself at so great a cost in the first place. Since we were at enmity
with him, showing contempt for his will, we deserved his wrath, not his
mercy. Yet he reconciled us to himself while we were enemies. Here is
the greatness of God's love.

The lesser wonder that provides greater assurance is that now we
shall be saved from the wrath of the last day. Our conversion experience
puts a solid historical basis under our assurance of final deliverance.
This is why "we also rejoice in God through our Lord Jesus Christ,
through whom we have now received our reconciliation" (v. 11).

The New Humanity (5:12-21)

No passage in this letter has suffered more distortion at the hands of
its interpreters than Romans 5:12-21. Much of the misunderstanding

has stemmed from a translation error in the Vulgate, a fourth-century Latin version of the Bible. In the last clause of verse 12 the Greek text has, "because all sinned." However, the Vulgate mistakenly rendered it, "in whom all sinned," with Adam regarded as the unnamed antecedent of "in whom."

Upon the basis of this translation error in the Vulgate, Augustine (AD 354-430) formulated his doctrine of original sin. He taught that all men were seminally present in the loins of Adam when he sinned. Thus he held that the whole human race sinned in Adam's sin. By virtue of our physical descent from Adam, we inherit his guilt. We are born guilty of original sin, according to Augustine.

Augustine taught further that infant baptism properly administered removes the guilt of original sin. However, if a child dies without being baptized, his soul is sent to limbo. For all eternity the child will experience natural happiness only and can never enjoy the supernatural happiness of heaven. Current Roman Catholic practice denies unbaptized infants burial in hallowed ground.

In the seventeenth century Johannes Cocceius proposed a different theory of original sin. He taught that God had entered into a covenant with Adam as the federal head of the human race. If Adam obeyed God, all mankind would receive eternal life; but if he disobeyed, all would be condemned to corruption and death. Since Adam sinned, God imputed his sin to all his descendants. This has been called the Federal Theory of Original Sin or the Theory of Condemnation by Covenant. It has greatly influenced the churches of the Reformed tradition. However, there is not one shred of evidence in the Bible that God ever entered into such a covenant with Adam. The theory was born in Europe, not Eden.

Such interpretations of Romans 5:12-21 have tended to ignore both its general and immediate contexts in the letter. In Romans 1:18 to 3:20 Paul set forth his doctrine of sin. Here he showed that all men, Gentiles and Jews alike, have become guilty, because all men have sinned (3:9,19,23). Human guilt derives from human sin; it is not inherited. Men are guilty because they have sinned, not because they were born. No interpretation of Romans 5:12-21 that obscures or refutes the plain teaching of Romans 1:18 to 3:20 can be correct. Is it not interesting that Paul managed to demonstrate the guiltiness of all men in this earlier passage without any reference to Adam?

The passage is set in the immediate context of Romans 3:21 to 5:11.

Here Paul set forth the gospel of the grace of God revealed through Jesus Christ his Son (3:21-31). Through faith in Jesus Christ sinful men may be justified before God or made right with him (3:24-25). Abraham himself was justified by faith and has become the father of all who believe (4:1-25). In Romans 5:1-11 Paul rejoiced in the benefits that have come to men through God's justifying grace. And in Romans 5:12-21 he continued to magnify God's grace by showing the vast scope of Christ's accomplishment on the cross. As Adam headed an old humanity characterized by sin and death, so Christ heads a new humanity characterized by righteousness and life. Indeed the theme of this passage is superabounding grace. Paul insisted that what mankind lost in Adam was more than regained in Christ.

Throughout the passage Paul used the rhetorical device of analogy. It is a powerful medium for overall impact. But it has more in common with the broad strokes of an artist's brush than it does with the fine lines of a draftsman's pen. Analogy is superb for producing a mural, whose perspective we enjoy from a distance. However, it leaves much to be desired for producing the exactness of close-up photography. For this reason, the interpreter who approaches this lyrical passage, so rich in its use of analogy, as though he were dealing with historical narrative is bound to garble its message.

From Adam to Moses (5:12-14).—Paul wrote, "Therefore as sin came into the world through one man and death through sin, and so death spread to all men because all men sinned" (v. 12). Observe that Paul never finished this sentence. Instead in verses 13-14 he dealt with a problem suggested by the final clause of verse 12. What about those who lived between Adam and Moses? What about the presence of sin in the world before the law was given? Paul asserted, "Sin indeed was in the world before the law was given, but sin is not counted where there is no law" (v. 13; see also 3:20; 4:15; Gal. 3:19).

Adam's sin was expressed in a deliberate transgression of God's commandment. It was not possible for those who lived between Adam and Moses to sin in this way. "Yet death reigned from Adam to Moses, even over those whose sins were not like the transgression of Adam, who was a type of the one to come" (5:14). This verse affirms that the old humanity headed by Adam was characterized by sin and death even during the time preceding the giving of the law. Also with its reference to Adam as a type of Christ, verse 14 provides a transition to the analogy in the following verses.

Adam and Christ: an analogy (5:15-19).—Five parallels between Adam and Christ are drawn in these verses. The first three are contrasts (vv. 15-17), and the last two are comparisons (vv. 18-19). The phrasing of these parallels is simplified in the following enumeration:

(1) A contrast between Adam's *trespass,* through which the many died, and the *free gift* of God's grace in Christ, which has abounded for many (v. 15).

(2) A contrast between the *condemnation* that followed Adam's one trespass and the *justification* that follows the free gift of God's grace coming after so many trespasses (v. 16).

(3) A contrast between the *death* that reigned through Adam's trespass and the much greater reign in *life* of those who receive the free gift of God's grace (v. 17).

(4) A comparison between the *condemnation* that came to all men through Adam's trespass and the *acquittal* that comes to all men through Christ's act of righteousness (v. 18).

(5) A comparison between the *disobedience* of Adam, through which the many were made sinners, and the *obedience* of Christ, through which the many will be made righteous (v. 19).

Paul wrote, "As by one man's disobedience many were made sinners, so by one man's obedience many will be made righteous" (v. 19). Yes, but we want to know how men were made sinners by Adam's disobedience. Was it because all men were seminally present in the loins of Adam when he sinned, and thus inherit his guilt (Augustine)? Was it because Adam as the federal head of the race cast the wrong vote in Eden (Cocceius)? No! There is no evidence for either of these theories of original sin in this passage. Indeed a study of both Genesis 3:1-24 and Romans 5:12-21 reveals that neither passage explains how the effects of Adam's sin were transmitted to his descendants.

But we do know much about the other half of the analogy, namely, how men are made righteous through Christ's obedience. We know that the death of Christ on the cross does not automatically grant all men a right standing with God. In Romans 3:24-25 Paul made plain that Christ's accomplishment on the cross avails for us only upon the basis of our faith in him. We do not inherit salvation because of what Christ has done. Rather by God's grace we receive salvation through faith in Christ.

We do not inherit salvation through Christ's obedience apart from our personal involvement in faith. Nor do we inherit condemnation through Adam's disobedience apart from our personal involvement in sin. Neither salvation nor guilt can be inherited.

It is noteworthy that there are Roman Catholic scholars today who are challenging their church's tradition regarding original sin. Thus Herbert Haag writes, "The idea that Adam's descendants are automatically sinners because of the sin of their ancestor, and that they are already sinners when they enter the world, is foreign to Holy Scripture."[7]

The triumph of grace (5:20-21).—Up to this point in his discussion of the two humanities headed by Adam and Christ (5:12-19), Paul made no mention of the law. Yet the giving of the law through Moses was a significant event in the national history of the Jews. Should not Paul have mentioned Moses alongside of Adam and Christ in his analogy? No! Moses did not belong in this exclusive company of the two Adams (see 1 Cor. 15:21-22, 45-49). Paul was speaking in terms of two orders of humanity: the old humanity marked by sin and death headed by Adam and the new humanity marked by righteousness and life headed by Christ. There is no third humanity headed by Moses.

Nevertheless, Moses was an important figure in God's redemptive plan. Through him, God gave the law for a specific purpose. Paul described it, "Law came in, to increase the trespass; but where sin increased, grace abounded all the more, so that, as sin reigned in death, grace also might reign through righteousness to eternal life through Jesus Christ our Lord" (vv. 20-21).

Through the giving of the law, God laid down a standard of that which was pleasing and displeasing in his sight. This standard had the effect of making sin visible as specific trespasses. Also it served to increase the trespass. Although this concept was shocking to devout Jews, Paul insisted that the law's purpose was to make sin obvious.

God's ultimate purpose in grace is to triumph over the reign of sin and death (v. 21). What a magnificent portrayal of the humanity-wide achievement of God's justifying work in Christ!

Changed Lives (6:1-23)

Freedom from sin (6:1-14).—In Romans 5:20 Paul stated that where sin abounded, God's grace superabounded. What wonderful news this is! It means that no matter how deep the stain of man's sin, the grace of God is greater. Thus there is hope for all, and men should praise God for his amazing grace.

Yet this great truth about the gospel was liable to grievous distortion by sinful men. They claimed that by sinning they were providing God with the opportunity to reveal the greatness of his grace. Paul described their error in two questions, "What shall we say then? Are we to continue in sin that grace may abound?" (v. 1). Already in Romans 3:5-8 Paul had dealt with a similar perversion of God's truth. Now he devoted the full force of his argument against those who claimed that they sinned to the glory of God. Outraged by this flagrant evil, Paul replied, "By no means! How can we who died to sin still live in it?" (v. 2).

In verses 3-4 Paul explained the Christian's death to sin by describing the meaning of baptism, "Do you not know that all of us who have been baptized into Christ Jesus were baptized into his death? We were buried therefore with him by baptism into death, so that as Christ was raised from the dead by the glory of the Father, we too might walk in newness of life." Surely no one who rightly understood the meaning of Christian baptism could hold so casual an attitude toward sin.

In many evangelical churches today people are invited to confess publicly their faith in Christ by walking an aisle and shaking hands with a pastor. But in Paul's day there were no Christian buildings with aisles for people to walk. Instead they made public their confession of faith in Christ by submitting to baptism. It is unlikely that Paul ever faced a situation in which one professed Christian faith and refused to be baptized. Baptism was both the time and the mode of confession whereby one made known his commitment in faith to Jesus Christ as Lord.

In baptism the believer is united with Christ in his death, burial, and resurrection. This reality is portrayed vividly through immersion. Lowered into the water, we are baptized into his death; we are buried with him. And the death that he accomplished was the once-for-all sacrifice for our sins (v. 10; see also Heb. 7:27; 9:12,26,28; 10:10; 1 Pet. 3:18). Raised from the water, we enter upon the new life of Christ's resurrection. Paul described it as a "walk in newness of life" (v. 4). The use of the term "walk" to describe conduct or manner of life was common to the Old Testament. Paul used it frequently (see Rom. 8:4; 13:13; 14:15; Gal. 5:16).

Paul did not say that the believer who has been buried with Christ in baptism has also experienced resurrection with him. This remained in the future: "If we have been united with him in a death like his, we shall certainly be united with him in a resurrection like his" (6:5). But he did affirm our present deliverance from bondage to sin: "We know that our old self was crucified with him so that the sinful body might be destroyed, and we might no longer be enslaved to sin" (v. 6; see Gal. 2:20; 6:14).

Interpreters differ regarding the meaning of the phrase translated "the sinful body" in verse 6. Most versions of the Bible render it as a reference to the sinful self, the old nature dominated by sin (KJV, RSV, NEB, TEV, NASB, NIV). However, T. W. Manson argues the corporate sense, "It is better to regard 'the body of Sin as the opposite of the 'body of Christ.' It is the mass of unredeemed humanity in bondage to the evil power. Every conversion means that the body of Sin loses a member and the body of Christ gains one."[8]

In describing the believer's actual condition, Paul used the indicative mood of several verbs: for example, "we who died to sin" (v. 2); "we were baptized into his death" (v. 3); "we were buried therefore with him by baptism into death" (v. 4); "if we have been united with him in a death like his," and we have (v. 5); "our old self was crucified with him" (v. 6); "he who has died is freed from sin" (v. 7); "if we have died with Christ," and we have (v. 8). Thus Paul declared the fact of the believer's death to sin.

Observe that the ethical commands in verses 11-13 are based upon these indicatives that describe our new condition in Christ. We are to consider ourselves dead to sin but alive to God in Christ Jesus (v. 11). We are to halt the reign of sin in our bodies, which demands obedience to its sinful lusts (v. 12). Rather than offering the parts of our body as ready instruments of wickedness, we are to offer ourselves to God "as men who have been brought from death to life" (v. 13). And all these imperatives reach their climax in the great promise, "Sin will have no dominion over you, since you are not under law but under grace" (v. 14).

In Christian discipleship the ethical imperatives are based upon our actual relationship to Christ. We are not confronted with a higher ethical code and then ordered to keep it in our strength only. The walk of grace is the day-by-day issue of the life of grace. Christian ethics are the expression of a relationship with Christ. If a Christian fails morally, it is not because the needed power was not *available.* It is because it was not *appropriated.*

Bondage to righteousness (6:15-23).—In Romans 6:14 Paul declared that Christians were no longer under law but under grace. This verse provides the transition to a restatement of the same problem mentioned in Romans 6:1, "What then? Are we to sin because we are not under the law but under grace?" (v. 15). Does grace encourage or permit the sin that the law forbids?

Evidently Paul had encountered Jewish opponents who maintained that the law was essential to keep believers from lapsing into pagan sins. Another possibility is that some believers felt that since they were under grace instead of law, they could sin without dire consequences. For there are people who turn to religion for some imagined immunity to the consequences of sin rather than a deliverance from its power. Such persons pervert the gospel of God's grace to encourage an ethic of license.

Paul used the analogy of slavery to combat a casual attitude toward sin. He reminded his readers that regardless of the religious claims they made, their real master was identified by the commands they obeyed. If they obeyed the commands of sin, then sin was their master, and death their destiny. If they obeyed the commands of righteousness, then righteousness was their master, and life their end (v. 16).

Paul expressed gratitude to God for the changed lives of his readers (v. 17). Formerly they had been the slaves of sin, but now they "have become slaves of righteousness" (v. 18). As slaves of Christ, Paul urged them to yield their "members to righteousness for sanctification" (v. 19).

The term translated "sanctification" occurs only two times in Romans, here and in verse 22. Not only is it a status provided by divine grace but also a goal toward which we move. In verse 19 "sanctification" is set over against "impurity" and "greater and greater iniquity." This suggests its moral or ethical sense. In verse 22 "sanctification" is the "return" or fruit of having been set free from sin (past action), and its end is "eternal life." Here the emphasis seems to be on Christian growth.

Romans 6:20-23 summarizes Paul's teachings on the moral consequences of justification by faith. He described the two masters, the two freedoms, the two returns or fruits, and the two destinies. The *two masters* are sin and righteousness. The *two freedoms* are mutually exclusive: the slave of sin is free from righteousness, and the slave of righteousness is free from sin. The *two returns* are shameful behavior and sanctification. The *two ends* are death and eternal life: "The wages of sin is death, but the free gift of God is eternal life in Christ Jesus our Lord" (v. 23).

Living in the Spirit (7:1 to 8:39)

Paul wrote in Romans 7:5, "While we were living in the flesh, our sinful passions, aroused by the law, were at work in our members to bear fruit for death." Here he was looking back to a time before he and his readers had become Christians. He described a life situation characterized by sin, law, and death. In a remarkable way this verse suggests the contents of Romans 7:7-25, for the same three elements dominate the longer passage.

Paul continued in Romans 7:6, "But now we are discharged from the law, dead to that which held us captive, so that we serve not under the old written code but in the new life of the Spirit." The introductory "but now" places this verse in strong contrast to the preceding one. Here Paul was describing their present circumstances as Christians. They were discharged from the law; they were dead to that which formerly bound them; and they were serving in the new life of the Spirit. Just as verse 5 suggests the content of Romans 7:7-25, so verse 6 suggests the content of Romans 8:1-39. The former passage discusses life under law, from which Christians have been set free. And the latter passage, one of the greatest in the Bible, elaborates upon life in the Spirit.

Paul's discussion of God's deliverance of sinful men by his grace reaches its climax in Romans 8.

Freedom from the Law (7:1-25)

Dead to the law (7:1-6).—In these verses Paul taught that Christians had died to the law. Thus the law no longer wielded authority over them.

The principle is laid down in verse 1 that the law exercises lordship over a man only so long as he lives. Death cancels the law's claim upon him.

To illustrate this principle, Paul introduced a marriage metaphor. A married woman is legally bound to her husband as long as he lives (v. 2). If she lives with another man while her husband survives, she will be called an adulteress. However, if her husband dies, she is free to marry another man (v. 3).

Then Paul applied the metaphor to the issue at hand, namely, the relation of the Christian to the law: "Likewise, my brethren, you have died to the law through the body of Christ, so that you may belong to another, to him who has been raised from the dead in order that we may bear fruit for God" (v. 4).

Admittedly, there is some awkwardness in Paul's application. In the illustration it was the husband who died, and the wife who was then free to marry another. But in the application it was the converts, represented by the wife, who died "to the law through the body of Christ." And having died, they were free to be joined to another, even to Christ.

The law and sin (7:7-25).—No passage in the Roman letter has been interpreted in more varied ways than this one. For instance, scholars differ regarding the nature of the personal references in these verses. Some think that they are autobiographical, providing intimate glimpses into Paul's religious experience. Others are equally sure that they are not autobiographical. Instead they assert that Paul adopted the "I" device as a general reference to all.

Even among those who agree that the passage is autobiographical, sharp differences remain. Some argue that Paul described here his experiences before becoming a Christian. That is, Paul the Christian was discussing life under law in the light of his former experience as Saul the Pharisee. Others are equally sure that Paul was sharing his present struggles as a Christian.

Still others propose a broad interpretation of Romans 7:14-25 that transcends the "then" and "now" periods of Paul's religious experience. For example, some feel that it describes the Christian who undertakes to live in his own strength alone without drawing upon the resources of grace. Or it may portray any man trying to do right but not "in Christ."

When dedicated scholars differ so widely in their understanding of a passage, we may suspect the tentative nature of the evidences. In such instances we may offer our opinions and engage in lively exchanges. But the evidences are too evenly divided for us to think we have the final word.

The following assumptions underlie the interpretation of Romans 7:7-25 ventured in these pages. (1) *Subject:* Paul discussed here the relation of the Christian to the law (vv. 1-6) and then showed the relation of the law to sin (vv. 7-25). A strong defense of the law as a God-given instrument characterizes his presentation. (2) *Background:* When Paul wrote these lines, he was a Christian missionary. Earlier he had been a Pharisee, zealous for the cause of Judaism. When he portrayed the effort to achieve a righteousness based on law, he drew upon his personal remembrances. To this extent the passage is autobiographical. (3) *Pre- or post-conversion:* When Romans 7:14-25 is read by itself, it sounds as though Paul were describing his present experience as a Christian. But when it is read in the total context of Romans 5:1 to 8:39, it seems to belong to his former experience as a Pharisee. Either interpretation is left with unresolved difficulties. However, the total impotence and abject despair of Romans 7:14-25 contrasts sharply with the triumphant affirmations of Romans 5:1-5; 6:1-11,14,17-19,22; 7:4-6; and 8:1-4.

Now we direct our attention to a brief analysis of this difficult passage. Paul began it with a question, "What then shall we say? That the law is sin? By no means!" (v. 7). This is a startling query. The necessity for raising it grew out of the preceding paragraph (vv. 4-6). There Paul taught that Christians had died to the law (v. 4; see 6:4, where he taught that they had died to sin). He described the former life in the flesh as a time when their sinful passions had been aroused by the law (v. 5). They had borne fruit for death. And he declared that Christians had been discharged from the law. Now they were free to serve in the new life of the Spirit rather than under the old written code (v. 6). In all these references the law was linked closely with sin. But Paul's answer to his self-imposed question was an emphatic, "By no means!" (v. 7). Any equation of the law with sin was a shocking distortion to him.

However, Paul saw a relation between the law and sin, and in verses 7-11 he sought to explain it. He cast his answer in the form of a personal testimony, "Yet, if it had not been for the law, I should not have known sin. I should not have known what it is to covet if the law had not said, 'You shall not covet' " (v. 7). This quote is the Tenth Commandment. A reading of Exodus 20:17 and Deuteronomy 5:21 will reveal that Paul omitted the objects of coveting enumerated in the texts. All that was necessary to his argument was that through the law he had come to a knowledge of sin (see Rom. 3:20; 4:15; 5:13; Gal. 3:19). This was an important function of the law.

Beyond this insight Paul indicated also that the law had stirred up the impulse to sin in him, "Sin, finding opportunity in the commandment, wrought in me all kinds of covetousness. Apart from the law sin lies dead" (v. 8). The word translated "opportunity" here and in verse 11 was used in a military context to designate a base of operations.

In Romans 5:20 Paul stated that the "Law came in to increase the trespass," and Paul bore witness to this strange work of the law. Yet he was careful to uphold its character, "The law is holy, and the commandment is holy and just and good" (v. 12).

Having shown how sin found a base of operations for death in the commandment, Paul raised a second question, "Did that which is good, then, bring death to me? By no means! It was sin, working death in me through what is good, in order that sin might be shown to be sin, and through the commandment might become sinful beyond measure" (v. 13).

Sin, not the law, was the culprit. And Paul affirmed that it was through the law that he came to realize how exceedingly sinful sin was. Suppose that sin could accomplish its work through sinful means only. That would be bad enough. But a particularly treacherous feature of sin is that it can achieve its evil ends through that which is good. It can take something as good as the law of God and accomplish death through it.

At this point Paul made a dramatic switch from past to present tenses as he continued to explain the relation between the law and sin: "We know that the law is spiritual; but I am carnal, sold under sin" (v. 14). This statement is powerful. Paul again defended the law. He affirmed that it was spiritual: God was its source, and it was spiritual in character. Thus the law was not the cause of death; sin was. And sin had its roots deep in carnal man, "living in the flesh" (v. 5). "Sold under sin" means bought and delivered to sin, as a slave to a master (NEB, "the purchased slave of sin"). This same verb was used in Matthew 18:25 to describe a debtor being sold into slavery.

A slave cannot act upon his own will. He is bound to obey his master. His noble desires will be overruled and crushed by the one who owns him. Through this metaphor of slavery Paul explained why he was unable to obey the law. As sin's slave, bought and paid for, he had to do his master's bidding. No matter how much he delighted in God's law, he was powerless to fulfill it. He felt compelled to do what he hated: "I do not do what I want, but I do the very thing I hate" (v. 15). "For I know that nothing good dwells within me, that is, in my flesh. I can will what is right, but I cannot do it. For I do not do the good I want, but the evil I do not want is what I do" (vv. 18-19).

In verses 21-25 Paul climaxed the account of the struggle in his life between the law of God and the law of sin. Both of these laws contended for mastery in him. Paul did not offer a neutral battleground. Instead he was deeply biased in favor of the law of God, in which he delighted. In his innermost self it appealed to him, and he aspired to fulfill it (v. 22). But the law of sin would not permit it. This dreadful alien law waged war against the law of God in Paul and took him captive (v. 23). As a prisoner he cried out for deliverance, "Wretched man that I am! Who will deliver me from this body of death?" (v. 24). And in the same breath he provided the triumphant answer: "Thanks be to God through Jesus Christ our Lord!" (v. 25).

The latter part of verse 25 seems anticlimactic: "So then, I of myself serve the law of God with my mind, but with my flesh I serve the law of sin." Moffatt's translation places these words at the end of verse 23 just before the cry of despair. Logic may be served by such a transposition of the text, but there is no manuscript evidence to support it. Thus it is better to permit the awkwardness to stand, regarding the sentence as a restatement of the conflict portrayed in verses 14-24.

Now look back over Romans 7:7-25 and ask: Did Paul describe here his struggle to achieve a righteousness based on law, aided by his reminiscences as a former Pharisee? Or, did he depict his present struggles as a Christian, having experienced a foretaste of the age to come but caught in the tensions of the present evil age? Or did he portray the experience of the Christian who relapses into legalism or of any man trying to do right but not "in Christ"?

The first of these explanations seems best to this writer. If the statement, "I am carnal, sold under sin" (v. 14) describes Paul's life as a Christian, what shall we make of Romans 6:14, "Sin will have no dominion over you, since you are not under law but under grace?" Should not Paul have written, "Sin will continue to have dominion over you, although you are not under law but under grace?"

It will not do to point to Galatians 5:17 in support of Romans 7:7-25 as a description of Paul's Christian experience. One wonders why the preceding verse, Galatians 5:16, is ignored in such references, "Now I say, keep on walking in the Spirit and under no circumstances will you fulfill fleshly lust" (author's translation). What a tremendous promise of victory for the Christian here and now! The following verse, Galatians 5:17, gives the reason for continuing to walk in the Spirit, namely, the ever-present tension between the old fleshly nature and the indwelling Spirit. Struggle and conflict are typical of Christian experience, but defeat and despair are not.

The New Life of the Spirit (8:1-39)

Twenty-one times in Romans 8 the Greek word for *Spirit* or *spirit* occurs. On one other occasion (v. 27) it is the understood subject of the verb "intercedes." (The RSV supplies the word "Spirit" in this instance, to make the thought flow of the verse more obvious.)

Of these twenty-two references, the Revised Standard Version capitalizes eighteen, indicating the Holy Spirit. The four exceptions are: (1) "your *spirits* are alive" (v. 10); (2) "the *spirit* of slavery" (v. 15); (3) "the *spirit* of sonship" (v. 15); and (4) "with our *spirit*" (v. 16). Yet two of these occurrences are translated as references to the Holy Spirit in other versions. (The KJV and TEV render the one in verse 10, "the Spirit is life." And the second reference in verse 15 is translated as follows: KJV, "the Spirit of adoption"; TEV, "the Spirit makes you God's children.") Thus there are at least eighteen and possibly twenty references to the Holy Spirit in this one chapter.

This fact means that there are more references to the Holy Spirit in Romans 8 than in any other chapter of Paul's letters. (1 Cor. 12 ranks second with twelve.) This is all the more remarkable in view of the fact that he used the term "Spirit" or "spirit" only five times in Romans 1—7 (1:4,9; 2:29; 5:5; 7:6). Here in this chapter we have Paul's fullest discussion of the new life of the Spirit. Observe the following features.

Deliverance from bondage (8:1-11).—The new life of the Spirit, made possible through faith in Jesus Christ as Lord, brings deliverance from the old bondage to sin and death. Thus Paul launched this portion of his letter with a mighty declaration of freedom, "There is therefore now no condemnation for those who are in Christ Jesus. For the law of the Spirit of life in Christ Jesus has set me free from the law of sin and death" (vv. 1-2).

Note the two laws mentioned here. One is the law of sin and death. Its work is described in Romans 7:14-25. It always lies close at hand, ready to challenge every desire to do right (7:21). It wages a relentless warfare until it has made a captive out of the one striving to fulfill God's law (7:22-23). It reduces him to impotence and wrings the cry of despair from his heart (7:24). But the cry of despair may become the threshold of hope. "For the law of the Spirit of life in Christ Jesus" (v. 2) breaks the dominion of the old law of sin and death. Through Jesus Christ men are set free.

Verse 3 tells how it happens. Once again Paul mentioned the limitation imposed on the law by the weakness of sinful men. (See Rom. 7:7,12,14.) Though God-given, the law cannot provide man with the moral power to meet its demands. But then God has acted in man's behalf; "God has done what the law, weakened by the flesh, could not do: sending his own Son in the likeness of sinful flesh and for sin, he condemned sin in the flesh" (v. 3).

Much of the gospel of the grace of God is found in this verse. Here

God is not the angry Father waiting to have his wrath against man appeased by the sacrificial intervention of a loving Son. Instead, God the Father acts in behalf of sinful man by sending his Son. And the manner of Christ's coming is described in the phrase "in the likeness of sinful flesh." This is the *incarnation.* Jesus Christ, the Son of God, became one with us in our humanity. He lived a real flesh-and-blood existence in our midst. Paul was careful to state this truth in a way that recognized the sinlessness of Christ. To come "in the likeness of sinful flesh" does not mean that he came as a sinner. Paul would have regarded such a statement as blasphemy. Instead Christ came "for sin." (See RSV footnote, "as a sin offering.") This is the *atonement.* Through his sacrificial death on the cross he achieved our deliverance by condemning sin in the flesh.

That is, flesh was regarded as the domain in which sin held sway. In his incarnation Christ invaded the realm of sin's tragic dominion. In his death on the cross he bore the full fury of sin's devastating power. And through the triumph of his death and resurrection, he condemned sin in the very area of its entrenchment. This is a legal metaphor. It means that God passed a sentence upon sin in the very area where it had staked out its claim.

He did this "in order that the just requirement of the law might be fulfilled in us, who walk not according to the flesh but according to the Spirit" (v. 4).

Paul did not teach that men, empowered by the Spirit, were saved by a keeping of the law. This teaching would still be justification by works. Rather he taught that God's requirement in the law had now become possible for man through the power of the indwelling Spirit. Working from within, the Spirit impels a conduct which the law, confronting from without, could not impose.

In verses 5-11 Paul drew several contrasts between the old life ruled by the flesh and the new life of the Spirit. (See Gal. 5:19-24.) Notice what he said about those whose lives were dominated by the old sinful nature. They "set their minds on the things of the flesh" (v. 5). They do so even though "to set the mind on the flesh is death" (v. 6). They are hostile to God, regarding him as an enemy. They do not submit to God's law; indeed, they cannot (v. 7). "And those who are in the flesh cannot please God" (v. 8). Yet a destiny for all eternity is at stake in this displeasure.

On the other hand, "Those who live according to the Spirit set their minds on the things of the Spirit" (v. 5). And to do so "is life and peace" (v. 6). They are indwelt by the Spirit of God, and this certifies that they belong to Christ (v. 9). Their bodies are dead, or possibly subject to death, because of sin. But the Spirit, who is life, imparts life to them, because they have been justified (8:10).[9] And they have an assured hope for the future based upon the resurrection of Christ from the dead (v. 11; see 1 Cor. 15:35-58).

In verses 9-10 Paul's thought flow moves from "Spirit of God" to "Spirit of Christ" to "Christ is in you." C. K. Barrett comments, "It is idle to seek a distinction between 'Spirit of God' and 'Spirit of Christ.' Each is a correct description of what Paul meant. The Spirit is the Spirit of God; and it is only through Christ that the Spirit is known and received."[10]

Sonship: an intimate personal relationship (8:12-17).—Those who have experienced the deliverance described in Romans 8:1-11 are under obligation not "to live according to the flesh" (8:12). For the old flesh life is opposed both in character and destiny to the new life of the Spirit (v. 13).

From this summation of the two ways—flesh and Spirit—Paul moved on to the theme of sonship. For through faith in Jesus Christ all believers "have been adopted into the very family circle of God" (v. 15, Phillips).

First, he described the *test* of sonship, "All who are led by the Spirit of God are sons of God" (v. 14). No evidence of our filial relationship to God exceeds this. A day-by-day response to the leading of the Spirit indicates the one to whom we belong. We follow the one we belong to. This is a more dependable criterion than our emotional highs and lows. Elation without obedience is a fraud.

Second, Paul pointed out the *privilege* of sonship, namely, the right to address God as "Abba! Father!" (v. 15). *Abba* is the Aramaic word for *father.* It is the intimate and endearing term by which the child in a Jewish home addressed his father. This term is found only three times in the New Testament: Romans 8:15; Galatians 4:6; and Mark 14:36. In the last reference Jesus used it as he called upon God in Gethsemane. No term serves better than this one to qualify the warm, personal relationship to God which his grace has made possible. It is the opposite of the spirit of slavery, with its cringing fear, which characterizes all legalistic religion.

"O Thou great Ineffable Other!" is for those who do not know God. But for those whom the Spirit of God has made sons, the more appropriate way to address God is "Abba! Father!"

The term translated "sonship" or "adoption" in verse 15 occurs only five times in the New Testament. All these are found in Paul's letters: Romans 8:15,23; 9:4; Galatians 4:5; and Ephesians 1:5.

Third, Paul indicated the *assurance* of sonship, "When we cry, 'Abba! Father!' it is the Spirit himself bearing witness with our spirit that we are children of God" (vv. 15-16). As God's children, we are "fellow heirs with Christ, provided we suffer with him in order that we may also be glorified with him" (v. 17). Observe Paul's emphasis here upon sharing Christ's sufferings. (See Phil. 1:29; 3:10; Col. 1:24.) These are not the adversities that come because of our common humanity, for example, illness, bereavement, or the loss of employment during a recession. Rather they are the sufferings incurred because we are following Christ.

Hope of God's ultimate triumph (8:18-25).—In the preceding verse Paul had introduced the thought of the Christian's participation in the sufferings and glory of Christ (v. 17). This suggests the theme for the present passage, namely, the relation between suffering and glory in Christian experience. In the explanation that Paul gave, we have one of the greatest statements on hope in the New Testament. Its sweep is so grand that it includes the destiny of the whole created order.

Paul began, "I consider that the sufferings of this present time are not worth comparing with the glory that is to be revealed to us" (v. 18). One has only to read such passages as 2 Corinthians 1:8-10; 4:7-12,16-18; 11:23 to 12:10 to realize how much Paul had suffered in Christ's service. Even while writing Romans, he was preparing to leave on a mission to Jerusalem that would endanger his life (Rom. 15:31). Yet he insisted that none of these trials deserved to be mentioned in the same breath with the coming glory.

In verses 19-22 Paul described creation's involvement both in man's bondage to sin and in his hope of redemption. Genesis 3:17-19 provides the background for this discussion. Notice what Paul said about the creation: (1) It eagerly awaits the revelation of the sons of God (v. 19). (2) It was subjected to futility, not willingly, but by the will of God, who subjected it in hope (v. 20). Some interpreters have proposed Adam or Satan as the agent of subjection, but if so, how does one explain the words "in hope"? (3) It is destined to be set free from enslavement to decay and to share in the glorious liberty of God's children (v. 21). (4) It groans and travails until now (v. 22).

In verses 23-25 Paul resumed his discussion of the lot of Christians amidst present trials. Like the creation, we too groan inwardly as we await the final day. We are grieved by the evidence in nature of man's enslavement to sin. We yearn for the full adoption as sons that shall take place in the resurrection. And we do so as those who have already received the first fruits of the Spirit. (See Lev. 23:15-21.) This is God's pledge of our complete triumph with Christ at the end. At present this is a hope (8:24) that we wait for with patience (v. 25).

"In the beginning God" (Gen. 1:1): this is the biblical teaching on creation. In the end God, too: this is the biblical teaching on the events of the end time or eschatology.

God is moving through history to the ultimate triumph of his redemptive plan in Jesus Christ. (See Eph. 1:9-10; Phil. 2:9-11.) The last authoritative word to be spoken in the consummation of Project Humanity will not emanate from the council chambers of ruling nations but from God. The only future there is, is God's future. And those who have been reconciled to God through faith in Jesus Christ are secure in its prospect.

Help in prayer through the Spirit's intercession (8:26-27).—Another bounty of the new life of the Spirit is at a point where we often need it most, namely, in our prayers. Due to our weakness, we often do not know how to pray as we ought (v. 26). This has been true also in times past of men who were greatly used by God. For example, Abraham prayed that Sodom be spared, but it was destroyed (Gen. 18:23-33). And no one is ever more compassionate than God. Again, Moses prayed for permission to enter Canaan, but it was not granted (Deut. 3:23-27). And God ever delights in giving to his children. Finally, Paul himself prayed for the removal of "a thorn . . . in the flesh," but God did not remove it (2 Cor. 12:7-10). Yet before God had finished with Paul in this painful experience, he was praising God for the affliction whose removal he had sought (2 Cor. 12:9-10).

Into this area of our need the Spirit comes with his ministry of assistance in our prayers (v. 26). The words translated "with sighs too deep for words" in verse 26 constitute a problem for the interpreter. As rendered in the Revised Standard Version, they apply to the Spirit. That is, the Spirit intercedes for us with unutterable (or possibly unuttered) groans. This seems to be the more natural sense of the verse. But *The New English Bible* translates it differently, "Through our inarticulate groans the Spirit himself is pleading for us" (v. 26). Here the worshipers are the ones who are sighing or groaning. Under some overwhelming emotional need, the work load of ordinary speech is exceeded. Thus the prayer burden can be expressed only through inarticulate sighs. The Spirit, however, understands the meaning of our sighs, and through them pleads our cause with the Father. And the God "who searches the hearts of men knows what is the mind of the Spirit, because the Spirit intercedes for the saints according to the will of God" (v. 27).

Our ignorance in prayer and the Spirit's intercession in our behalf are clearly taught in the passage. But the phrase in question allows either interpretation.

God's overruling care (8:28-30).—One of the greatest promises in the Bible is found in this passage, "We know that all things work together for good to them that love God, to them who are the called according to *his* purpose" (v. 28, KJV, author's italics).[11]

Notice that this verse does not say that all things work together for good for all people. Many men live in an open rebellion against God. Others live in a complete indifference to his claims upon them. To suppose that their revolt works to their good is to propose a moral contradiction. For sin in the hearts of men is real for God. On the contrary, in Romans 6:23 Paul said, "The wages of sin is death."

The passage specifies those for whom the promise of this verse holds when it says, "to them that love God, to them who are the called according to *his* purpose" (v. 28, KJV). The first clause sounds as though the initiative rested with man. That is, as a consequence of man's love for God, all things work together for good. But the second clause acknowledges that the initiative in our conversion is taken by God. He calls us by his grace and according to his purpose. To God's extended grace we respond in faith. For those who respond to God's love with love, and for those who answer God's call in faith, the promise is assured.

But what is the "good" that is promised? The answer is found in verse 29, "Those whom he foreknew he also predestined to be conformed to the image of his Son, in order that he might be the first-born among many brethren." God's will for every Christian is a maximum family resemblance to our Elder Brother. He seeks to order our lives to achieve this lofty purpose.

Evil and tragedy are real in the world, and sometimes God's people suffer crushing sorrow. We must refrain from attributing to the will of God that which is not true to Christ's revelation of him. God is not responsible for terrible crimes; sinful men and women are. They occur because God's will is flagrantly transgressed. And the transgressing of the will of God can never be the carrying out of his will.

Yet God's love and resources are so great that he can overrule in the tragedies we suffer. Whether sorrows and tears or joys and laughter, he can work through them all to make us increasingly like Jesus Christ. And that is what God's grace is all about. The larger the family of God's children, the greater the honor to his Son in being the firstborn.

In verse 30 Paul bridged eternity past and future with his majestic summation of God's redemptive purpose. Notice the four mighty spans in this bridge. *Predestination* is God's purposive grace at work before the foundation of the world. *Calling* and *justification* are God's grace confronting us and making us right with himself in the midst of history. *Glorification* is the ultimate triumph of God's grace in the consummation. Paul regarded our future glorification with Christ as so certain that he described it with a past tense, as though it had already happened.

Assurance of salvation (8:31-39).—Predestination, calling, justification, glorification: these great terms comprehend the scope of God's redemptive purpose. Having set them forth in stair-step fashion in verse 30, Paul asked, "What then shall we say to this?" (v. 31). His answer has provided the grandest passage on Christian assurance in the Bible. Observe the solid foundation of our confidence.

First, our assurance is based upon the heavy investment that God has already made in our redemption (vv. 31-32). As evidence that God is for us, Paul pointed back to the cross, "He who did not spare his own Son but gave him up for us all, will he not also give us all things with him?" (v. 32). Here is a confidence based upon what God has already done, and so it is neither an idle speculation nor an unsupported hope. Golgotha was God's firm commitment to us, not a trial run. (See Rom. 5:6-11.)

Second, our assurance is based upon God's acquittal and Christ's continuing intercession for us (vv. 33-34). A courtroom scene is imagined. The question is asked, "Who shall bring any charge against God's elect?" (v. 33). This is a challenge that might well cause us to tremble, except for one thing: "It is God who justifies" (v. 33). And none can press further charges against those whom God has acquitted. Another question is posed, "Who is to condemn?" (v. 34). The answer is, "It is Jesus Christ, who died, yes, who was raised from the dead, who is at the right hand of God, who indeed intercedes for us" (v. 34, see RSV footnote). The only one who could condemn us is actually pleading our cause at the right hand of God.

Third, our assurance is based upon God's great love for us in Christ, which guarantees that nothing will be able to separate us from him (vv. 35-39). After enumerating the various calamities that have assailed God's people (vv. 35-36), Paul claimed, "We are more than conquerors through him who loved us" (v. 37). This statement provides the background for one of the greatest affirmations of faith in God of all time, "I am sure that neither death, nor life, nor angels, nor principalities, nor things present, nor things to come, nor powers, nor height, nor depth, nor anything else in all creation, will be able to separate us from the love of God in Christ Jesus our Lord" (vv. 38-39). In this sentence Paul included the full range of existence (death and life) and all hostile supernatural forces (angels, principalities, powers). He included all uncertainties of time (things present and things to come) and every reach of space (height and depth). Then, lest any source of threat be overlooked, he added, "nor anything else in all creation" (v. 39).

This testimony of assurance was shared with a church within a decade of facing persecution under Nero in Rome. And shortly after writing it, Paul left for Jerusalem, where an attempt was made on his life. (See Acts 21:27-36.)

The Destiny of Israel
9:1 to 11:36

At the beginning of this letter Paul had declared that the gospel was rooted in God's dealings with Israel (1:1-3). Israel was the chosen people. Deuteronomy 7:6 reads, "You are a people holy to the Lord your God; the Lord your God has chosen you to be a people for his own possession, out of all the peoples that are on the face of the earth." (See Ex. 4:22; Ezek. 20:5; Isa. 43:10-13; Acts 13:17.) Yet at the time that Paul wrote to Rome the Jewish people by and large had rejected the gospel. They stood outside of God's deliverance through faith in Jesus Christ. Now then, how can one reconcile God's election of Israel with her rejection?

Here is a problem that Paul could not ignore in his exposition of the revelation of God's righteousness, which is the theme of Romans (1:17). Its treatment must not be regarded as a digression or an appendix. Paul needed to show that there was no conflict between the gospel of God's grace and his promises to Israel. He did it by affirming his personal concern (9:1-5), God's sovereignty (9:6-29), Israel's responsibility (9:30 to 10:21), and Israel's hope (11:1-36).

To avoid distortions, one should read Romans 9—11 as a unit. Unless Romans 9:6-29 is seen in the light of Israel's responsibility in Romans 9:30 to 10:21, it seems harsh. Until Romans 9:6 to 10:21 is seen in the light of Israel's hope in Romans 11:1-36, it seems bleak. These three chapters begin with a lament (9:1-5), but they end with a doxology (11:33-36).

Paul's Lament (9:1-5)

Ultimate Compassion (9:1-3)

When Paul thought of his people and their alienation from God, he felt an overwhelming grief. Placing himself under a solemn oath, he disclosed his unceasing anguish in their behalf (vv. 1-2).

How deep was Paul's compassion for his people? He stood ready to forfeit his own hope in Christ if only it could benefit them: "I could wish that I myself were accursed and cut off from Christ for the sake of my brethren, my kinsmen by race" (v. 3). Our word *anathema* is a transliteration of the Greek word that Paul used in expressing his dreadful wish (translated "accursed"). It occurs only six times in the New Testament, five of which are in Paul's letters. (See v. 3; 1 Cor. 12:3; 16:22; Gal. 1:8-9; Acts 23:14.)

This is compassion in its ultimate form. Love knows no greater expression than this. Being the apostle to the Gentiles meant no lessening of Paul's concern for the salvation of his fellow Jews.

The Advantage of the Jews (9:4-5)

In verses 4-5 Paul listed several advantages of the Jews that made their rejection all the more tragic: (1) *They were Israelites.* This name signified a special relation to God (Gen. 32:28; Eph. 2:12). (2) *They were adopted as sons* (Ex. 4:22-23; Deut. 14:1; 32:6; Hos. 11:1; Jer.

31:9). (3) *They had the glory of God.* This was the divine splendor of
light that descended when God visited his people (Ex. 16:10; 24:16-17;
29:43; 33:18-23; 40:34; 1 Kings 8:10-11). In later literature this reality
of God's presence or nearness to his people was called the *Shekinah.* (4)
They had the covenants. God had pledged a special relationship with
Abraham, Isaac, Jacob, and the people at Mount Sinai (Gen. 15:18;
17:2; 26:2-5; 35:9-15; Ex. 24:8). (5) *They had the law.* This provided or
made possible a revelation of the will of God that exceeded anything
known to the Gentiles (Rom. 2:17). (6) *They had the worship services of
the Temple.* (7) *They had the promises.* In Romans 4:13-25 Paul had
discussed God's promise to Abraham and his descendants. The promises
of God pointed ahead to the coming of the Messiah and his kingdom.
(8) *They were descendants of the patriarchs.* "To them belong the
patriarchs, and of their race, according to the flesh, is the Christ. God
who is over all be blessed for ever. Amen" (v. 5). Jesus Christ was born a
Jew (1:3; see also Gal. 4:4-5; Matt. 1—2; Luke 1—2; 3:23-38).

Yet with all these advantages of God's special blessings throughout
their history, the Jews did not acknowledge Jesus as the Messiah. As a
people, they rejected him. (See John 1:11.) And Paul's heart was heavy
with grief, because his own people disdained God's deliverance through
faith in Jesus Christ.

God's Sovereignty (9:6-29)

The Israel Within Israel (9:6-13)

Paul insisted that the word of God had not failed, though most of
Israel had not believed in Jesus Christ. This was true because God's
promises were not intended for all who could boast of racial descent
from Abraham. Rather they belonged to the children of promise, who
were the true descendants of Abraham. They constituted the Israel
within Israel (vv. 6-8).

Ishmael was as much the son of Abraham as was Isaac. Yet no Jew
considered the Ishmaelites to be children of God's promise to Abraham.
Instead the covenant relationship continued through Isaac.

Perhaps some Jew would point to the obvious fact that though Ishmael and Isaac were fathered by Abraham, they had different mothers.
Ishmael's mother was Hagar, the slave woman, whereas Isaac's mother

was Sarah, the freeborn wife of Abraham. Thus the Jew would account
for God's choice of Isaac over Ishmael.

However, Paul's next reference to God's purposive selection at work
in history permitted no such explanation. In verses 10-13 he described
God's choice of Jacob over Esau. In this instance both sons had the same
father and mother. Rebecca conceived both by Isaac (v. 10). Furthermore, God chose Jacob, the younger twin, rather than Esau before they
were even born (v. 11). Thus the selection could not have been based
upon the doing of right or wrong.

The Absolute Freedom of God (9:14-18)

Admittedly, God's action with respect to Jacob seems unfair. Paul
anticipated a possible charge of injustice against God, but quickly dis-
missed it (v. 14). He cited God's message to Moses, "I will have mercy
on whom I have mercy, and I will have compassion on whom I have
compassion" (v. 15). This citation of Exodus 33:19 has its original setting in the aftermath of the worship of the golden calf (Ex. 32:1-10).
Apart from God's mercy, his judgment would have consumed the idolatrous people immediately. Thus it is not the exercise of man's will or his
striving that compels God to withhold his judgment; it is his mercy (v.
16).

The opposite of showing mercy to the sinner is hardening the heart of
the sinner. As God's word to Moses was an instance of the former, so his
dealings with Pharaoh provided an example of the latter (v. 17). Paul
attributed both the bestowal of mercy and the hardening of the sinner's
heart to God's sovereign will: "So then he has mercy upon whomever he
wills, and he hardens the heart of whomever he wills" (v. 18).

The nature of grace requires absolute freedom on God's part.

The Israel Beyond Israel (9:19-29)

This is an exceedingly difficult teaching, and Paul felt the necessity of
permitting his imaginary opponent to press his argument still further:
"You will say to me then, 'Why does he still find fault? For who can
resist his will?' " (v. 19). To this pertinent question he gave a sharp
rebuke (v. 20). He affirmed the right of the potter to fashion vessels of
his choosing out of the same lump of clay before him. This was true
whether the vessels were made for exalted or menial use (v. 21).

Against this background Paul asked the lengthy hypothetical question
in verses 22-24 that suggests his answer to the problem of Israel's status

and destiny. Observe the following: (1) The unbelieving Jews are vessels of wrath, whom God has endured with much patience (v. 22). Romans 9:30 to 10:21 explains this, reaching its climax in the words of Isaiah 65:2 in the final verse, "Of Israel he says, 'All day long I have held out my hands to a disobedient and contrary people' " (10:21). A passage like this shows that Paul never intended his metaphor of the potter to deny man's responsibility before God. One does not extend pleading hands to a pot! (2) Through the revelation of his wrath and power in his dealings with the unbelieving Jews, God intends to make known the riches of his glory (v. 23). He overrules the disobedience of Israel, and calls into being vessels of mercy, including Gentiles as well as Jews (v. 24). Romans 11:1-32 explains this, reaching its climax in verse 32, "God has consigned all men to disobedience, that he may have mercy upon all." Once again, the vessels Paul described in chapter 11 were capable of responding to God's call. (See 11:20,22-23.)

Paul cited Hosea 2:23 and 1:10 in Romans 9:25-26 to confirm that God's redemptive plan included Gentiles as well as Jews. And he cited Isaiah 10:22-23 and 1:9 in Romans 9:27-29 to confirm that only a remnant of Israel would be saved.

Israel's Responsibility (9:30 to 10:21)

Had Paul's discussion ended with Romans 9:29, Israel's rejection would have seemed a decision of the sovereign God. Any questioning on man's part was rebuked as impudence (9:20). But it did not end there. Without any thought of contradiction Paul continued his discussion of the same theme from the standpoint of Israel's responsibility. Thus we see that the Israel whom God rejected was the Israel who had rejected God.

The Stone of Stumbling (9:30-33)

In these verses Paul pointed to another apparent unfairness regarding Israel and then offered an explanation. That is, the Gentiles who did not pursue righteousness have attained it by faith, whereas Israel, having pursued the righteousness based on law, fell short of it (vv. 30-31). Paul explained why Israel's pursuit of a right standing with God had failed. It was because they did not seek it through faith. They imagined that they could make themselves right with God by keeping the law. Thus they refused to believe in Jesus Christ. He was the stumbling stone over whom they had tripped and fallen. Paul cited a combination of Isaiah 28:16 and 8:14 to support his charge. (Compare 1 Pet. 2:6-8.)

The Two Ways of Seeking a Right Standing with God (10:1-13)

As in Romans 9:1-5, Paul expressed again his concern for the salvation of his people (v. 1). He bore witness to the Jews' zeal for God but lamented that it was not enlightened (v. 2). Ignorant of the right standing with God made possible through faith, they sought to establish their own right standing with God by keeping the law (v. 3). They failed to recognize that Christ put an end to the law as a way of achieving righteousness for everyone who believes (v. 4; 3:21; Gal. 3:19 to 4:7).

An alternate view of Romans 10:4 claims that Christ is the "end" of the law in the sense of its "aim" rather than its "termination." Thus the law has its meaning and fulfillment in Jesus Christ.

There is a strange reference to bringing Christ down from heaven and up from the dead in verses 6-7. The background for this passage is Deuteronomy 30:11-14, where Moses was speaking to the people about keeping God's commandment. Yet Paul's words in verse 7 differ from all known forms of Deuteronomy 30:13. Probably Paul meant to assert that Christ already had achieved all that was necessary for our salvation. Nothing remained now but to confess him as Lord and to receive salvation through him by faith (vv. 8-9). Some scholars believe that verses 8-9 contains an early confession of faith.

As there is no distinction between Jew and Greek in sinfulness (3:22-23), so there is none between them in salvation (v. 12; 3:29-30). The paragraph ends with the quotation of Joel 2:32, declaring the good news that "every one who calls upon the name of the Lord will be saved" (v. 13).

A Disobedient and Contrary People (10:14-21)

This passage is difficult. Paul's flow of thought is sometimes hard to follow. The support he gave to his argument by the Old Testament quotations is not always obvious. Yet the main thrust of the passage is plain: namely, Israel is responsible for her rejection. She herself has rejected the word of God that was near her (v. 8).

Observe the three objections that Paul's imaginary opponent raised in defense of Israel.

Israel lacked messengers from God (10:14-17).—The words "calls upon" in Joel 2:32, quoted in the preceding verse (v. 13), become the first step in a series of four questions in verses 14-15. The implication in these questions is that Israel was not at fault in her failure to believe God's word, because she lacked preachers of the gospel. But Paul quoted Isaiah 52:7 in verse 15 and Isaiah 53:1 in verse 16 to refute the objection. God had been faithful in sending his messengers, but Israel did not heed the gospel they preached (v. 16).

Israel lacked the opportunity to hear (10:18).—This seems to be a restatement of the first objection. Paul phrased the question and then cited Psalm 19:4 to refute it. In its original setting this quotation referred to the heavenly bodies that declare the glory of God and proclaim his handiwork. Paul applied it to the preaching of the gospel.

Israel lacked understanding of God's message (10:19-21).— Otherwise she would have believed it. The fault lay in the obscurity of God's word. Had Israel understood the gospel, she would have received it.

Paul quoted from both Moses (the law) and Isaiah (the prophets) to refute this objection. First, he cited Moses in Deuteronomy 32:21 (v. 1). His reason for doing so is not clear. Perhaps he pointed to the Gentiles' acceptance of God's message to deny the Jews' claim that it was too hard to understand. Second, he cited the bolder statement in Isaiah 65:1 (v. 20). God said that he was found by a people who were not even seeking him. How much more then he should have been found by Jews, who admittedly had a zeal for God (v. 2).

The real explanation for Israel's rejection of the gospel was not a lack of understanding. It was an obstinate rebellion against God. Paul confirmed this judgment by a quotation of Isaiah 65:2, "But of Israel he says, 'All day long I have held out my hands to a disobedient and contrary people' " (v. 21).

Israel's Hope (11:1-36)

Had Paul's discussion of Israel's destiny ended with Romans 10:21, her prospects would have been dismal indeed. Paul anticipated such a conclusion in his next question, "I ask, then, has God rejected his people? By no means!" (v. 1). The two preceding chapters must make way for the hope that Paul described in Romans 11. Here Paul discussed the remnant of Israel (vv. 1-10); the evangelization of the Gentiles and Israel's jealousy because of the success of the Gentile mission (vv. 11-24); and the eventual turning of Israel to Christ (vv. 25-36).

The Remnant (11:1-10)

Paul followed up his emphatic denial that God had rejected his people by pointing to himself as a Christian Jew (v. 1). Thus the rejection of Israel was partial rather than total. There was a remnant of Jewish believers, and Paul was one of them.

Paul found evidence for his teaching about the remnant in the experience of Elijah (vv. 2-4). At a time of national crisis the prophet had complained to God that he was the only one who had remained faithful (v. 3; see 1 Kings 19:10,14). Whereupon God told Elijah that he had seven thousand men who had not bowed the knee to Baal (v. 4; see 1 Kings 19:18).

Making his application, Paul affirmed, "So too at the present time there is a remnant, chosen by grace. But if it is by grace, it is no longer on the basis of works; otherwise grace would no longer be grace" (vv. 5-6). As the seven thousand in Elijah's day were God's remnant, so were the Christian Jews of Paul's time. And their promise bespoke God's grace rather than man's achievement.

What about the rest of the Jews? They failed to obtain the right standing with God they had sought on the basis of works of law (v. 7; 9:31-32). Instead they were hardened. Paul supported this charge against the unbelieving Jews by appealing to the Old Testament. In verse 8 he described the hardening in terms taken from Isaiah 29:10 and Deuteronomy 29:4. And in verses 9-10 he quoted Psalm 69:22-23.

The Salvation of the Gentiles (11:11-24)

The description of the hardening of unbelieving Israel in the preceding verses drew from Paul a further question, "So I ask, have they stumbled so as to fall? By no means!" (v. 11). His answer in verses 11-12 reveals the main points of his discussion in the rest of the chapter: (1) Through the trespass of Israel, salvation has come to the Gentiles. (2) Through the salvation of the Gentiles, Israel will be provoked to jealousy. (3) Through the inclusion of Israel, great blessings will come to all. Not only was the rejection of Israel *partial* but also it was *temporary*.

In verses 13-16 Paul addressed his Gentile readers in his role as an apostle to the Gentiles. He told them he magnified his ministry, in order to make the Jews jealous, and thus save some of them (vv. 13-14). In this way Paul had an indirect ministry to the Jews also. He expressed enthusiasm for what the acceptance of the Jews would mean for the world (v. 15). He introduced the dedication of the first fruits of dough and the root of the tree to support his hope of the ultimate salvation of Israel (v. 16; see Num. 15:17-21).

In verses 17-24 Paul used the allegory of the olive tree to warn the Gentiles against boasting over the Jews. In the allegory the olive tree represents true Israel. Unbelieving Jews are the natural branches that have been broken off. Believing Gentiles are the wild olive branches that have been grafted in. Notice the reasons Paul gave to the Gentiles for not boasting over the Jews: (1) They should remember that they are wild olive shoots who were engrafted (vv. 17-18). (2) They should understand that the natural branches were broken off because of their unbelief and take heed not to presume upon God (vv. 19-22). (3) They should realize that God has the power to graft the natural branches into the olive tree, provided that they do not persist in their unbelief (vv. 23-24).

The Salvation of Israel (11:25-36)

Paul continued, "Lest you be wise in your own conceits, I want you to understand this mystery, brethren: a hardening has come upon part of Israel, until the full number of the Gentiles come in, and so all Israel will be saved" (vv. 25-26).

This is an amazing declaration regarding Israel's destiny. Only a few verses before, Paul had described Israel in terms of two groups: the elect remnant and the rest who were hardened (vv. 7-10). But here Paul announced boldly that all Israel would be saved (v. 26).

What was the basis for such a claim? Paul described it as a "mystery" (v. 25), a special insight into God's saving plan given him by revelation. The content of the disclosure was that a hardening had come upon a part of Israel "until the full number of the Gentiles" had come to Christ. Then Israel would be saved (v. 26).

As you may expect, interpreters differ widely in their understanding of this difficult passage. Here are some of the main proposals: (1) All men, both Gentiles and Jews, will ultimately be saved. None will be lost. This universalist point of view appeals to the so-called "larger hope" of verse 32. (2) "All Israel" means the church, the new Israel of

God. This explanation spiritualizes the term "Israel," rather than regarding it as a designation of the Jewish people. (3) The conversion of Israel will take place at the time of the Lord's return. Variations of this view may be found in the premillennial and postmillennial explanations of the events associated with the second coming of Christ. (4) "All Israel" indicates a great turning of Israel to Christ, without specifying the conversion of every individual Jew. That is, the meaning of the term "all Israel" must take its cue from the sense of "the full number of the Gentiles." As the latter did not indicate that every individual Gentile would be saved, so the former did not mean that every individual Jew would be saved. But Paul envisioned a great turning to Christ on the part of the Jewish people. Furthermore he likely expected all this to take place during his lifetime (13:11-12).

Of the four interpretations of verses 25-26 listed above, the last one seems most probable to this writer, though not without difficulties.

In verses 26-27 Paul confirmed the "mystery" just described with a combination of quotations from Isaiah 59:20-21 and 27:9. In verse 29 he reaffirmed his hope for the Jews by his insistence that "the gifts and the call of God are irrevocable." As the Gentiles had been disobedient and then received mercy, so the disobedience of the Jews would also yield to God's mercy (vv. 30-32).

With this summation of God's gracious ways with men, Paul burst into praise. He magnified the depth of God's riches, wisdom, and knowledge. No one could search out his judgments nor track his ways (v. 33). Isaiah 40:13 was quoted to show that God's wisdom was so great that he needed neither counselors nor brain trusts (v. 34). Job 41:11 was used to show that the riches of God were so great that he required no financial backing (11:35).

"Source, Guide, and Goal of all that is—to him be glory for ever! Amen" (v. 36, NEB).

The Pattern of Discipleship
12:1 to 15:13

Through the first eleven chapters of Romans we have followed Paul's presentation of the gospel. First, he described the sinfulness of men

(1:18 to 3:20). Then he showed how God had moved through the death
and resurrection of Jesus Christ, his Son, to save them (3:21 to 8:39).
Next he discussed the problems relating to the destiny of Israel (9:1 to
11:36). And now we come to the last major division of the letter (12:1 to
15:13), where Paul applied the gospel to everyday living.

In this lengthy passage on the pattern of discipleship Paul dealt with
the following subjects: the call to commitment (12:1-2); charismatic
gifts (12:3-8); personal relationships (12:9-21); Christian citizenship
(13:1-7); the primacy of love (13:8-10); the end of the age (13:11-14);
and unity amidst differences (14:1 to 15:13).

Call to Commitment (12:1-2)

The Greatest Sacrifice: Your Very Selves (12:1)

Paul used the language of the altar to urge his readers to costly commitment. He told them to present their bodies as a sacrifice to God. He
may have meant "bodies" in a literal sense as he did in Romans 6:12-13.
Or he may have used the term in a wider sense to refer to the whole person (NEB, "your very selves").

Three qualities describe the Christian's sacrifice: (1) It is *living.* This
concept may provide a contrast with the dead bodies of animal sacrifices. Or it could denote the new life that the believer possesses in Christ
(6:1-14; 2 Cor. 5:17; Gal. 6:15). (2) It is *holy.* The Christian is set apart
for and belongs to God. (3) It is *well-pleasing to God.* That sacrifices
are offered to God is not enough. The offerings made must be acceptable to him.

Paul said that such a sacrifice was the Christian's "spiritual worship"
(KJV, "reasonable service"). The word translated "spiritual" may also
mean "rational." It occurs only twice in the New Testament: 1 Peter
2:2 and here.

The Greatest Motivation: the Mercies of God (12:1)

No greater demand can be made of any Christian than that he climb
upon God's altar as a living sacrifice. The motivation, therefore, must
be equal to the demand. Only one exists. Paul appealed to it in the
words, "by the mercies of God."

The word "therefore" in verse 1 is significant. It reaches back to
include the whole account of God's unfolding mercy to sinful men in the

first eleven chapters. If gratitude to God for his mercies does not compel our devotion to him, nothing will. No greater appeal can be made.

Paul never degraded the gospel by diluting its call to commitment.

The Greatest Threat: the Pressure to Conform to This World (12:2)

The word translated "world" is literally "age." Behind it lies the Jewish concept of the two ages: the present evil age (Gal. 1:4) and the glorious age to come. Christians are described as those "upon whom the end of the ages has come" (1 Cor. 10:11). We live as men and women of two ages: *witnessing* to the one that is dying and *walking* toward the one that is dawning.

But the world does not like this. It imposes a relentless pressure upon Christians to conform to its dying ways and values. The only world we know found the matchless Son of God intolerable. It nailed him to the cross. The world often reserves its bitterest scorn, not for its reprobates, but for those who take the lordship of Jesus Christ most seriously in their lives.

Thus Paul urged the Roman Christians to resist the efforts of a sinful age to shape them according to its mold. The verb translated "be conformed" carries this idea. First Peter 1:14 is the only other passage in the New Testament in which this verb occurs.

The Greatest Discovery: the Will of God (12:2)

The opposite of being conformed to this age is to "be transformed by the renewal of your mind." The purpose of this transformation is that we may be able to "prove what is the will of God." The word translated "prove" means to discern through testing. In 1 Peter 1:7 it describes gold that was "tested" by refining fires.

The greatest discovery of all is the will of God. It is good, well-pleasing, and complete. And the place from which to seek it is atop the altar as a living sacrifice.

Charismatic Gifts (12:3-8)

The Nature of the Church: One Body in Christ (12:3-5)

Paul urged his readers not to think too highly of themselves (12:3; see Gal. 6:3-5). Evidently pride posed a threat to the unity of the church in Rome. The specific cause of the pride is not identified. Yet verse 3 leads directly into a discussion of spiritual or charismatic gifts. Perhaps this was a divisive issue, even as it had been earlier in Corinth. (See 1 Cor. 12—14.)

Paul described the church as "one body in Christ" (12:5; see 1 Cor. 12:27). As such, it has many members, who perform different functions. But these functions, however diverse they may be, are related to each other as are functions of the parts of the body.

All members of the body depend upon each other. They are joined by an interdependence of both function and disability. When all parts function normally, the body enjoys health. If any member malfunctions, the body suffers a loss. (See 1 Cor. 12:14-26.)

The Variety and Use of Charismatic Gifts (12:6-8)

The charismatic gifts are abilities or powers which the Spirit of God bestows upon all believers to equip them for service. They are an important part of the gospel of grace. We are *saved* by grace; we *grow* by grace; and we are *endowed* by grace. Here it is: salvation, growth, and service—an experience of God's grace from beginning to end.

We are no more left to our own resources in Christian service than we are in salvation and growth. As "one body in Christ" a church is a group of baptized believers who worship, fellowship, witness, and serve to the glory of God. This body has a shape. It is not a random assembly of individual believers. The Spirit of God equips each member to function as a meaningful part of the body. We have tended to neglect the New Testament teaching of the church as a "gifted body." (See also 1 Cor. 12:4-31; Eph. 4:11-12; 1 Pet. 4:10-11). For the spiritual gifts are not only *functional* but also *congregational.*

We have "gifts that differ according to the grace given to us" (12:6). In verses 6-8 Paul enumerated seven forms of Christian ministry vital to the congregational witness in a community. They are: prophecy, service, teaching, exhortation, giving, ruling (better than "he who gives aid," RSV), and acts of mercy. For each of these related functions, there is a qualifying spiritual gift.

Personal Relationships (12:9-21)

General Instructions (12:9-13,15-16)

Love must be genuine, not a form of role-playing. (In verse 9 the word translated "genuine" is literally "without hypocrisy.") We are to "hate what is evil, hold fast to what is good" (v. 9). One cannot do the latter without doing the former. This insight is one that permissiveness never grasps. Brotherly love is to prevail, and we are to "outdo one another in showing honor" (v. 10).

In zeal we must not lag behind. We are to "be aglow with the Spirit" (v. 11). The word translated "be aglow" was used in Acts 18:25 to describe Apollos.

"Serve the Lord" is plain enough (v. 11). Some manuscripts have "season" instead of "Lord." In Greek the spelling of the two words is similar. If "season" is correct, then Christians are urged to meet the challenge of an age fast drawing to a close.

Rejoicing in hope, enduring in tribulation, and continuing in prayer are likewise enjoined (v. 12). Also Christians should contribute to the needs of the saints and practice hospitality (v. 13). Both are forms of sharing.

Love has a capacity to identify with others in their joys or sorrows (v. 15). To identify with persons in sorrow is sometimes easier than to identify with them in their joys, since we never envy the griefs of others.

Love seeks harmony in all personal relationships (v. 16). It readily associates with the lowly. (See RSV footnote, "Give yourselves to humble tasks.") Freedom from conceit helps to make this possible.

When Wronged by Others (12:14,17-21)

Paul wrote, "Bless those who persecute you; bless and do not curse them" (v. 14). This is not a quotation of the words of Jesus in Matthew 5:44 and Luke 6:28, but it reflects the same attitude.

We are not to repay evil for evil (v. 17). Again this sounds like the teaching of Jesus against retaliation in Matthew 5:38-42. Rather we must "take thought for what is noble in the sight of all" (v. 17). This quotation is from Proverbs 3:4. It reflects the concern frequently expressed by Paul about the impressions that Christians make upon unbelievers. (See 1 Thess. 4:12; 1 Cor. 6:1; 2 Cor. 8:20-21.)

Insofar as it depends upon us, we are to "live peaceably with all" (v. 18). However, at times our best efforts end in failure. Another person may choose to interpret our actions in the worst possible way and then refuse to be reconciled. This unjust treatment hurts. It even tempts us to renewed resentment. We may be helped, however, by realizing that God never withholds his peace from us because of another's wrong.

In no instance are we to take vengeance into our own hands. Instead we are to give place to the wrath of God (v. 19). Only he knows enough to make the punishment fit the wrong. In verse 20 Paul quoted Proverbs 25:21-22, "If your enemy is hungry, feed him; if he is thirsty, give him drink; for by so doing you will heap burning coals upon his head." This obscure metaphor likely means that such noble conduct will produce remorse in one's enemy and lead him to repent. Thus one resists the temptation to be overcome by evil and instead overcomes evil with good (v. 21).

The world at its worst returns evil for good. The world at its best returns good for good and evil for evil. But the follower of Jesus Christ is commanded to return good for evil.

Christian Citizenship (13:1-7)

Some Historical Factors

This brief passage on a large subject has often been lifted out of its context. We may avoid the most common distortions of Paul's teaching by keeping the following historical factors in mind:

(1) In AD 49 the Roman emperor Claudius expelled the Jews from Rome. As noted in the Introduction, the banishment may have been caused by disturbances in the Jewish quarters of the city over the Christian claim that Jesus was the Christ.

(2) Following the death of Claudius in AD 54, Nero, his successor, relaxed the edict. As many Jews returned to Rome, it was imperative that further hostilities be avoided.

(3) This is the only passage of its kind in Paul's letters. Thus we may surmise that the Roman Christians needed special instructions regarding their civic responsibilities. Perhaps some harbored a rebellious spirit, while others were indifferent to the common duties of all citizens.

(4) At this time in Judea the relations between the Jews and their Roman rulers were growing worse. Already Jewish militants were pursuing a course that would lead to the suicidal revolt against Rome in AD 66-73. Soon after sending his letter to Rome in AD 55-56, Paul left for Jerusalem with the relief offering.

(5) Up to this time there had been no official persecution of Christians in the Roman Empire. Local or sporadic outbreaks of violence against them were led by pagans or Jews. In some instances Roman officials had provided protection to Christian missionaries. For example, Paul ap-

peared before Gallio in Corinth (Acts 18:12-17).

(6) Paul's teaching on civic duties was set in the context of his expectation of the Lord's return soon (13:11-14; see 1 Cor. 7:25-31 on marriage).

Duties to the State (13:1-7)

With this historical setting in mind, we note Paul's instructions to his readers regarding the governing authorities.

Christians must be subject to rulers (13:1-2).—The authority of the state is grounded in the will of God (v. 1). To resist rulers is to resist what God has appointed and to incur judgment (v. 2).

Christians must recognize the function of rulers (13:3-5).—Rulers maintain order in society by rewarding good conduct and punishing wrongdoing (v. 3). In wielding the sword (the power of life and death), rulers are God's servants who execute his wrath upon wrongdoers (v. 4). Not only the fear of punishment but also the demands of conscience require submission to them (v. 5).

Christians must support rulers (13:6-7).—They are obligated to pay taxes and revenues to support the governing authorities. Also they owe them respect and honor (v. 7).

That Paul did not qualify his statements troubles many modern readers. For example, he did not discuss the limits of Christian obedience, the possibility of the moral justification of revolution, or the duties of rulers to their subjects. But in just 144 words of original text he laid down the basic instruction: Christians, like all others, are to obey their rulers. (See Mark 12:13-17; 1 Tim. 2:1-2; Tit. 3:1-2; 1 Pet. 2:13-17.)

Primacy of Love (13:8-10)

The previous paragraph dealt with the God-invested authority of the state, submission to rulers, the payment of taxes, and respect for those in public office. This paragraph expands to describe the Christian's obligation to all men, namely, love (v. 8). All the commandments are summed up in the one sentence, "You shall love your neighbor as yourself" (v. 9).

Since love does no wrong to a neighbor, it is the fulfilling of the law (v. 10).

End of the Age (13:11-14)

Paul used the metaphor of night and day to describe the relative progress of the two ages. The present age of darkness was already far spent (v. 12). It was time for Christians to arouse from their sleep, "For salvation is nearer to us now than when we first believed" (v. 11; see 1 Thess. 5:4-7). Paul was thinking of the culmination or climax of our salvation at the return of Jesus Christ. For the salvation we know now by faith awaits the last day for its full deliverance. Paul declared that God's glorious day was at hand. It was time to "put on the armor of light" (v. 12; see Eph. 6:13-17; 1 Thess. 5:8; 2 Cor. 6:7).

No conflict exists between Christian hope and ethics, as has sometimes been charged. On the contrary, the hope of the Lord's return creates a healthy ethical tension in one's life. Positively this means that one walks "becomingly as in the day" (v. 13). Paul urged, "Put on the Lord Jesus Christ, and make no provision for the flesh, to gratify its desires" (v. 14; see Gal. 3:27; Eph. 4:24; Col. 3:10). Negatively it means that we cast off the works of darkness (v. 12; see Gal. 5:19-21; Eph. 4:22; Col. 3:8). In verse 13 Paul named six works of darkness: reveling, drunkenness, debauchery, licentiousness, quarreling, and jealousy.

Unity Amidst Differences (14:1 to 15:13)

Does unity in a church require a uniformity of conviction at every point of belief and practice? Are all the things we believe and do of equal importance, and therefore obligatory upon all members? Do differences in religious and cultural backgrounds have any influence upon our understanding of Christian discipleship? If so, how far can one group go in imposing its distinctive scruples upon others who do not share them?

These are not idle questions, for they introduce the problem Paul addressed in the most extensive ethical passage in the Roman letter. Earlier he had found it necessary to warn the Gentile Christians not to boast over the Jews (11:17-24). Engrafted branches should not make root noises! Then he spoke out against pride and arrogance, reminding the members of the church that they constituted "one body in Christ" (12:3-5). He urged his readers to live in harmony with one another and to avoid haughtiness and conceit (12:16). And now he directed his attention to a specific issue that was threatening the unity of the church in Rome.

The Problem (14:2,5,21)

Throughout the passage Paul spoke of two groups of believers, whom he designated as the "weak" and the "strong." He mentioned three points at which they held sharp differences of opinion: (1) the eating of meat (v. 2); (2) the observance of special days (v. 5); (3) the drinking of wine (v. 21). The weak shunned meat and ate vegetables only, whereas the strong ate anything. They felt that their liberty in Christ rendered obedience to ancient dietary codes meaningless. The weak attached special religious value to certain days, whereas the strong esteemed all days equally valuable. They felt that Christian faith exempted them from following ancient religious calendars. The weak abstained from wine, whereas the strong drank it. They felt that abstinence was as meaningless as the observance of outmoded food laws.

Interpreters struggle to identify these two groups more precisely. In view of the earlier evidence of tension between Jewish and Gentile believers, many conclude that the Jewish believers are the "weak," whereas the Gentile believers are the "strong." Although the law did not require a vegetable diet, it did specify certain meat as unclean, for example, pork. Also the law gave strict instructions for slaughtering animals, and these instructions had been honored by devout Jews for centuries. The sale of meat from animals used in pagan sacrifices further complicated matters. (See 1 Cor. 8—10.) Thus many Jewish Christians may have become vegetarians rather than run the risk of eating forbidden or unclean meat. They believed that the ancient dietary code was binding upon all followers of Christ. In this they revealed that they were weak or immature Christians.

A similar attitude prevailed with the Jewish Christians regarding the observance of an ancient calendar which specified certain days of particular religious significance. These likely included the Jewish festivals and keeping the sabbath as a holy day. When Gentile Christians refused to share their convictions regarding food laws and a religious calendar, the Jewish believers criticized them. In return the Gentile believers scorned their Jewish brothers for their lingering legalism. Thus the unity of the church was threatened by differences of opinion regarding matters not essential to salvation.

But other interpreters point to the insistence upon abstinence from wine (14:21) and rightly claim that this was not a Jewish practice. Thus identifications of the two groups are proposed which are less precise and more hypothetical. For example, the "weak" represented a curious mixture of Judaistic and gnostic tendencies, or even more generally, a blend of Jewish and pagan elements that cannot be clearly defined.

Christian Guidelines (14:1 to 15:13)

It is interesting to observe what Paul did *not* suggest as the best way to resolve the problem in Rome. For example, he did not command the church to assemble to remove the "weak" from church membership. Earlier he had given such an instruction to the church in Corinth regarding a man who was sexually immoral (1 Cor. 5:3-5). Some know only the strategy of confrontation and dismissal. Nor did he attempt to draft a definitive statement regarding the particular issues in question and then demand the compliance of all as a test of orthodoxy. For some regularly confuse uniformity with unity. They do not realize that uniformity is rarely achieved without coercion, itself a denial of unity.

No! As Paul sought the leadership of the Spirit of God in his counsels to the church in Rome, he felt led to suggest a different course. Rather than creating a law, he offered some Christian guidelines designed to achieve unity amidst differences. He seemed more concerned that the "weak" and the "strong" learn to live together than that all the differences between them be removed.

Notice three principles that Paul laid before his readers.

Judgment is God's right, not man's (14:1-12).—God has welcomed both the "weak" and the "strong" into his household. By grace both are his servants. As servants, neither has the right to pass judgment upon the other. That right belongs to God alone (v. 4). Instead each should act in the light of his own convictions regarding the religious scruples in question (v. 5). Both the observer and the nonobserver of the food laws and special days may have an equal desire to honor the Lord (v. 6).

But the "weak" must stop passing judgment on his brother who does not share his convictions at such points. And the "strong" must stop scorning his brother who clings to them (v. 10). Rather both need to realize that they will stand before the judgment seat of God, to give an account of themselves to him (vv. 10-12; see 2 Cor. 5:10).

The "weak" are characterized by lingering legalism. They tend to be harsh in their criticism of those in the church who do not share their opinions. Whereas the "strong" are characterized by the knowledge that

Jesus Christ has put an end to all religious legalism. They rejoice in their liberty in Christ. But the "strong" may be tempted to look down upon their less mature brothers.

One *flouts*; the other *flaunts*—both are wrong!

Love requires self-limitation for the sake of others (14:13-23).—Here Paul directed his counsel primarily to the mature. They were able to bear the greater responsibility for healing the breach in fellowship. Thus he urged them to "decide never to put a stumbling block or hindrance in the way of a brother" (v. 13). To be sure, no meat is unclean in itself (see Mark 7:14-23), "but it is unclean for any one who thinks it unclean" (v. 14). One cannot violate his conscience, even when inadequately instructed, without great harm to himself.

If the mature ignore the influence of their conduct on the immature, they no longer walk in love (v. 15). For love willingly foregoes all liberties that would cause a brother to stumble (v. 21; see 1 Cor. 8:13). After all, the mature have two satisfactory courses open to them, whereas the immature have only one. With regard to meat, the mature may choose either to eat or to abstain without incurring any harm. However, the immature can choose only to abstain without wounding their conscience.

God's reign is not fulfilled in food and drink laws, but rather in "righteousness and peace and joy in the Holy Spirit" (v. 17). Therefore, we are to "pursue what makes for peace and for mutual upbuilding" (v. 19). The believer whose faith and actions are in harmony before God is blessed indeed (v. 22). For "whatever does not proceed from faith is sin" (v. 23).

Follow Christ's example of forbearance (15:1-13).—Paul linked himself with the "strong" in his appeal that they "bear with the failings of the weak" (v. 1). By seeking our neighbor's good instead of pleasing ourselves, we follow Christ's example of forbearance (vv. 2-3). Think of all the instances of self-denial in the life and teachings of Jesus (Mark 8:34; John 13:3-5). Yet Paul made no appeal to the earthly ministry of Jesus. Instead he supported his claim regarding Christ by quoting from Psalm 69:9. Having done so, he affirmed the value of the Scriptures for our instruction and hope (v. 4). And in the benediction of verses 5-6 Paul prayed that his readers live in such harmony with each other and in such accord with Christ that they would be able to glorify God with one voice.

How are the Roman Christians to welcome one another? Paul instructed, "as Christ has welcomed you, for the glory of God" (v. 7). Indeed, Christ's welcome of both Jewish (v. 8) and Gentile (vv. 9-12) believers is to be the measure of their acceptance of each other.

A second benediction brings the main body of the letter to an end in Romans 15:13.

Conclusion

15:14 to 16:27

Travel Plans (15:14-33)

Goal of Paul's ministry (15:14-21).—In bringing his letter to a close, Paul expressed his confidence in the character and competence of his readers (v. 14). He admitted a boldness in the way he has written to remind them "on some points" (v. 15). But as a minister of Christ to the Gentiles, he was eager that the offering of the Gentiles as a sacrifice to God would be acceptable (v. 16).

In seeking to win obedience from the Gentiles, Paul had preached the gospel from Jerusalem to Illyricum, a province bordering the Adriatic Sea (vv. 18-19). It was his particular ambition to preach the gospel in pioneer areas which had never heard it (15:20-21).

Plans to visit Rome (15:22-29).—At the beginning of his letter Paul had mentioned his oft-delayed plans to visit Rome (1:10-15). Now at the end he repeated them. Only here he disclosed a further plan not mentioned earlier, namely, the evangelization of Spain. Feeling that his work in the East had drawn to a close, he wanted to visit Rome briefly and then press on to Spain (vv. 22-25). Obviously he had written this letter to gain the support of the Roman church for his mission to the West.

For the present, however, his visit to Rome and points beyond had to be postponed. First, he had to accompany the delegates from the Gentile churches to Jerusalem with the relief offering (vv. 25-28; see also Acts 20:3-6; 24:17). As soon as this mission had been completed, Paul would visit Rome en route to Spain (15:29).

Requests for prayer (15:30-33).—Concerned about the trip to Jerusalem, Paul asked his readers to pray: (1) that he would be delivered from unbelievers in Judea (v. 31); (2) that his ministry in behalf of the poor believers in Jerusalem would be acceptable to them (v. 31); (3) that God would permit him the refreshment of his anticipated visit to Rome (v. 32).

The study of Acts 21:15 to 28:31 provides insights regarding God's answer to these prayer requests.

Final Words (16:1-27)

Commendation of Phoebe (16:1-2).—As indicated earlier (see Introduction), some believe that chapter 16 was not a part of Paul's original letter to Rome. Rather Paul wrote it as a letter of commendation of Phoebe to the church at Ephesus. However, none of the arguments advanced in support of this opinion is conclusive. With good reason, many continue to regard all sixteen chapters as Paul's letter to the church at Rome.

Phoebe, a deaconness of the church at Cenchreae, may well have been the bearer of this great letter to Rome (v. 1). She had been a faithful helper of many in the work of the gospel. Now Paul wanted the Roman Christians to receive and help her in any way she needed (v. 2).

Personal greetings (16:3-16,21-23).—Twenty-six people are named in verses 3-16. Furthermore Paul revealed an intimate knowledge of their family relationships and Christian service. Some have argued that Paul could not have known so many in a church he had never visited. Thus they point to Ephesus.

However, the many who are named here may have been Paul's friends and converts in other places who had since moved to Rome. For the very reason that he was a stranger to Rome, he would have been eager to greet the ones he knew.

Those named in verses 21-23 were with Paul when he was writing the letter, likely from Corinth.

Warning against those who create dissensions (16:17-20).—It is impossible to identify these creators of dissensions with any particular group. They opposed the doctrines that had been taught to the Roman believers (v. 17). They were both self-serving and smooth-talking (v. 18). They were to be noted and avoided by the church (v. 17). And the alerted believers could rest assured that the God of peace would soon crush Satan under their feet (v. 20; see Gen. 3:15). This will take place at the end of the age, which Paul expected soon (see 13:11).

Benediction (16:25-27).—Some manuscripts support verse 24, "The grace of our Lord Jesus Christ be with you all. Amen" (KJV). However, the Revised Standard Version, New English Bible, New American Standard Bible, New International Version, and other modern translations place this verse in the footnotes.

In the original text verses 25-27 constitute one long, involved sentence, that reads differently from the usual Pauline benediction. It focuses upon "the revelation of the mystery which was kept secret for long ages" (v. 25). The mystery, of course, is God's disclosure of his salvation through Jesus Christ. The objective in preaching the gospel to all nations is "to bring about the obedience of faith" (v. 26). Thus, "to the only wise God be glory for evermore through Jesus Christ! Amen" (v. 27).

Notes

Grateful acknowledgment is hereby made to Convention Press for permission to draw upon Dr. MacGorman's work, *Romans: Everyman's Gospel,* copyrighted in 1976.

1. Irenaeus, "Against Heresies," III, iii, 2, 3, in *The Anti-Nicene Fathers,* ed. Alexander Roberts and James Donaldson, I (New York: Charles Scribner's Sons, 1925), 415-16.

2. Related to this issue are the textual difficulties regarding the various benedictions (15:33; 16:20,24,25-27) and the original ending of the letter. Those desiring to study these technical aspects of the Roman letter are urged to consult the more extensive commentaries included in the bibliography.

3. W. Marxsen, *Introduction to the New Testament,* trans. G. Buswell (Philadelphia: Fortress Press, 1968), pp. 99-101.

4. Forms of the verb *to save* occur in only eight passages in Romans. In six of these (5:9-10; 9:27; 10:9,13; 11:26) the verb is in the future tense, emphasizing the climactic aspect of our salvation at the final judgment. Romans 8:24 and 11:14 are the exceptions.

5. A. M. Hunter, *The Epistle to the Romans, Torch Bible Commentaries* (London: SCM Press Ltd., 1955), p. 31.

6. *The Apocrypha of the Old Testament,* ed. Bruce M. Metzger (New York: Oxford University Press, 1965), p. 187.

7. T. W. Manson, "Romans," in *Peake's Commentary on the Bible,* ed. Matthew Black (London: Thomas Nelson and Sons, Ltd., 1962), p. 943.

8. As noted earlier, translations of Romans 8:10 vary considerably. Some find here a reference to a human spirit (RSV, NEB, NASB, NIV). Others regard it as a reference to the Holy Spirit (KJV, TEV).

10. C. K. Barrett, *A Commentary on the Epistle to the Romans, Harper's*

New Testament Commentary (New York: Harper & Brothers, 1957), pp. 158-59.

11. The RSV follows a variant reading that has "God" as subject of the verb: "We know that in everything God works for good with those who love him, who are called according to his purpose." It has strong support.

1 CORINTHIANS

Introduction

For Paul's most complete statement of the gospel of God's grace, we must turn to Romans. But for his most extensive correspondence with a single church, we must turn to the Corinthian letters.

Perhaps this was because no other church gave Paul as much trouble as the one in Corinth. Sometimes it is the child who has the most difficulty growing up who demands most of the parents' attention. This certainly was true of the church in Corinth in its relationship to Paul.

Here a number of his converts struggled with the responsibility of being the people of God in the midst of a pagan city. Some of them had been saved out of lives of deepest degradation (6:9-11), and the temptation to lapse into old vices remained strong. All of them lived under the relentless pressures of a pagan society which sought to conform them to its corrupt ways. Thus 1 Corinthians provides the most intimate disclosure of the inner life and workings of an early congregation to be found in the New Testament.

Before turning to the text of the letter, we need to give further attention to some matters of historical background.

The Importance of Corinth

In the Graeco-Roman world of Paul's day Corinth was a city whose importance was exceeded only by Rome, Alexandria, and Ephesus. In 27 BC it had become the capital of the province of Achaia. The Roman proconsul lived there. Thus Corinth was important politically.

It also enjoyed a commercial advantage. A glance at a map reveals its favorable location on a narrow neck of land which joined the Peloponnesus to the Greek mainland. Cenchreae, about eight miles to the east, was its port on the Saronic Gulf; and Lechaeum, less than two miles to the west, was its port on the Gulf of Corinth. To avoid the dangerous voyage around the southern tip of Greece, the cargos of many large ships were transported between these two harbors. Small boats were dragged from one port to another on a device of rollers. Today a canal, begun by Nero about AD 67, but not completed until 1893, provides passage. Located thus on the main sea route between the East and West and on the only land route between northern and southern Greece, the city's commercial importance was assured. In Paul's day it was the most affluent city in Greece. Many different races and nationalities filled its ports, places of amusement, business houses, and streets.

Also many pagan temples and shrines thrived in the city. If you visit the site of ancient Corinth today, you will still marvel at the seven stately columns of the temple of Apollo, dating from the sixth century BC. A temple of Asclepius, the popular god of healing, was there. Terra-cotta replicas of various parts of the body have been found in the ruins, the votive offerings of patients grateful for their healing. The devotees of Serapis and Isis occasionally provided processions in the streets. Yet the most important cult in Corinth was that of Aphrodite. It was her temple that occupied the summit of the Acrocorinth, the imposing mountain that dominated the city. Originally the Greek goddess of love and beauty, her worship had assumed the shocking degradations associated with the worship of the Phoenician Astarte, notorious in the Old Testament. Thus Strabo reported that in Old Corinth, the one destroyed by the vengeful Romans in 146 BC, there were a thousand cult prostitutes connected with her shrine.

In fact, at a time when public morality throughout the Roman empire was at a low level, Corinth was noted for its moral depravity. The very name of the city became a verb which meant "to live an immoral life." Its many taverns and easy access to prostitutes had given rise to a proverb among seafaring men, "Not for every man is the voyage to Corinth."

The Preaching of the Gospel in Corinth

To this prosperous and grossly immoral city, the apostle Paul came to preach the gospel of Jesus Christ about AD 50 or 51. As a result of his Spirit-empowered witness, aided notably by Aquila and Priscilla, the church in Corinth was born. Most of its members were Gentiles and from the lower classes (1 Cor. 1:26-31; 7:18-24; 8:7; 11:21-22; 12:2). The story is told in 1 Corinthians 2:1-5 and Acts 18:1-18. Important historical data leading up to the ministry in Corinth may be found in 1 Thessalonians 2:1 to 3:10.

Paul's Correspondence with the Church in Corinth

Our 1 Corinthians was not Paul's first letter to the church in Corinth. According to 1 Corinthians 5:9 Paul had written an earlier letter. It was probably lost, though some scholars believe that a portion of it has been preserved in 2 Corinthians 6:14 to 7:1. Nor was 2 Corinthians Paul's next letter to the church. Intervening 1 and 2 Corinthians was a letter of harsh rebuke. Evidently Paul had made an emergency trip from Ephesus to Corinth which was not recorded in the book of Acts (2 Cor. 2:1; 12:14; 13:1). That visit had turned out badly for Paul. Upon his return to Ephesus he wrote a stern letter to them. Either it has been lost or, as many scholars affirm, a large portion of it has been preserved in 2 Corinthians 10—13. Later in Macedonia, having received good news of Corinth from Titus (2 Cor. 7:5-7), Paul wrote 2 Corinthians, at least chapters 1—9. At any rate, Paul wrote a minimum of four letters to Corinth, and what we have of them constitutes the largest body of his writings in the New Testament.

Date and Purpose of 1 Corinthians

According to 1 Corinthians 16:8-9 Paul was in Ephesus when he wrote this letter. We will be reasonably accurate if we date it AD 54 or 55. But why did he write it? For an answer we turn briefly to the letter itself. In 1 Corinthians 1:11 Paul mentioned the visit of "Chloe's people." She may have been a Christian woman who maintained places of business in both Corinth and Ephesus. Some of her people told Paul about the factions that were destroying the unity of the church. Thus he addressed this problem in the first four chapters. They may also have reported the moral laxity and lawsuits among the members, to which Paul devoted attention in chapters 5—6.

However, beginning in 1 Corinthians 7 it is obvious that Paul was responding to a letter that raised questions about marriage and divorce (7:1-40), eating food offered to idols (8:1 to 11:1), charismatic gifts (12:1 to 14:40), the relief offering for Jerusalem (16:1-4), and the plans of Apollos (16:12). This letter was likely brought to Paul by Stephanas, Fortunatas, and Achaicus (16:17). These may well have confirmed and elaborated upon the troubled circumstances in Corinth. For Paul wrote also about the problem involving the participation of unveiled women in public worship (11:2-16), the disgraceful way in which the Lord's Supper was being profaned (11:17-34), and the denial of the resurrection (15:1-58).

What we have in 1 Corinthians then is a practical discussion of the typical problems Christians encounter as they seek to be the people of God in a pagan society. It has a special message for Christians of any age who cannot tell the difference between *involvement* with the world and *entanglement* by the world.

Salutation

1:1-9

Christian Greetings (1:1-3)

As always Paul followed the ancient letter form in the salutation. He placed his name first as the writer. Then he addressed those whom he was writing and offered the customary prayer for grace and peace in their behalf.

Some notable expansions in this salutation merit further attention. First, Paul identified himself as one whom God called "to be an apostle of Christ Jesus" (v. 1). This was not a vocation that Paul chose; it was a divine summons that he obeyed. No man can be more tragically out of place than the man in the gospel ministry by *choice* rather than by *response.*

Second, Paul designated his readers as "the church of God which is at Corinth" (v. 2). They have been "sanctified in Christ Jesus" (v. 2); that is, they have been set apart as belonging to God. This suggests the real meaning of the term "saints." They are not cherubic phantoms who somehow always photograph with a halo—a sort of third gender. Rather, they are those who through faith in Jesus Christ have been separated unto God. They belong to him and are at his disposal. And they have a vital kinship "with all those who in every place call on the name of our Lord Jesus Christ" (v. 2).

Third, Paul magnified the grace and peace of God in his prayer for the Corinthian believers (v. 3). These two qualities sum up the essence of the Christian gospel. Grace is the unmerited favor of God and the expression of his love that we could never deserve. God mediates his salvation to us by grace through Jesus Christ, his Son. (See Eph. 2:8-10.) Peace is the consequence of the grace of God in the lives of all who confess Jesus Christ as Lord.

Thanksgiving (1:4-9)

The thanksgiving also was a customary feature of the ancient letter. Like the personal address and prayer, it regularly preceded the main body of the letter.

Thanking God for you (1:4).—Just think of the sticky problems that Paul knew he would have to discuss as he began writing this letter. Yet here he was thanking God for his gift of grace to the Corinthians.

Paul had borne testimony to Christ in this city whose wickedness was proverbial in the ancient world. The Spirit of God had confirmed the simple preaching of the gospel with great power, and a number of the Corinthians had been saved. And when Paul recalled this marvelous demonstration of God's power to save, he readily expressed his gratitude.

In every way enriched (1:5-7).—Paul specified two ways in which his readers had been made rich, namely, "with all speech and all knowledge" (1:5). These are distinctive spiritual gifts or endowments. (See 1 Cor. 12:8; 13:1-2.) More than one form of speech is described in this letter. For instance, in 1 Corinthians 14:1-25 Paul compared the relative value of two speaking gifts: prophesying and speaking in tongues. Each is a different kind of utterance, but both are spiritual gifts.

On the other hand, the gift of knowledge relates to the understanding of the gospel. Paul used the word translated "knowledge" ten times in 1 Corinthians, six times in 2 Corinthians, and only seven times in his other letters. Some scholars regard this as important evidence that Paul wrote 1 Corinthians to refute a new gnostic interpretation of the gospel.

Both of these gifts, speech and knowledge, were subject to abuse in Corinth.

Anticipating the Lord's return (1:7-8).—The early Christians believed not only that Jesus Christ had died for their sins and had arisen from the dead, but also that he would return soon in triumphant glory. Apparently Paul believed this climactic event would occur during his lifetime. (See 15:51-52; 1 Thess. 4:16-17.) Thus the Corinthians were described as eagerly awaiting "the revealing of our Lord Jesus Christ" (v. 7).

Paul assured his readers that Jesus Christ would sustain them to the end (v. 8). This was a frequent theme in Paul's writings as he pointed men to One who not only saved but kept. (See Rom. 5:9-11; 8:31-39.) In the judgment that follows Christ's return, they would be found guiltless.

The fellowship of Christ (1:9).—The remarkable hope expressed in verse 8 rests upon a sure foundation, namely, the faithfulness of God. He is its unfailing guarantee.

The word translated "fellowship" describes sharing with Christ. The call of God is a call to relationship and participation in the life of his Son. There is no higher destiny, here or hereafter.

Now look back over this salutation (vv. 1-9) and observe what it reveals about God's call to us in Jesus Christ:

(1) It sets us apart for God, making us saints (v. 2).

(2) It relates us to the vibrant community of those in every place who call upon the name of Christ (v. 2).

(3) It is an expression of God's grace and brings peace (v. 3).

(4) It always enriches and endows us (vv. 5,7).

(5) It is mediated through testimony borne to Christ (v. 6).

(6) It plants a sustaining hope and assures an ultimate deliverance (vv. 7-8).

(7) It rests upon the faithfulness of God and invites us to share in the life of Christ (v. 9).

Church Divisions

1:10 to 4:21

Paul began the main body of his letter by directing attention to the problem of divisions in the church (1:10 to 4:21). We do well to take note of the priority that he gave to this subject. Not only did he address it first but also at greater length than any other issue except charismatic error in chapters 12—14.

There is a solid reason for this priority. Above all else, the gospel is a love story. It describes God's love for a sinful human race that led Jesus Christ, his Son, all the way to the cross. Only love can tell this story well. Unlove may use the right words, but the vibrations will be wrong. And people feel vibrations while hearing words. Thus the church whose fellowship is broken by divisions gives the lie to the message of God's reconciling love that it is charged to proclaim and live.

The last thing the world needs is further instruction or example in how *not* to live together peaceably. It has already written the manual on that theme. And the church that reflects more of a sinful world's power to divide than of Christ's power to unite has lost its right to address it.

Report from Corinth (1:10-17)

Quarreling Among You (1:10-12)

These verses reveal the reason for Paul's concern. Some of Chloe's people, possibly her servants, had brought Paul word about strife in the church at Corinth. We know little about Chloe, but she was well enough known to give validity to Paul's source of information.

Paul specified the form of divisions or factions in the church, "What I mean is that each one of you says, 'I belong to Paul,' or 'I belong to Apollos,' or 'I belong to Cephas,' or 'I belong to Christ'" (v. 12).

Evidently the Corinthian converts felt themselves qualified to pass judgment on the relative merits of the apostles. They even divided themselves into rival groups, replete with the rallying cries of their favorites. Paul had planted the gospel in Corinth (3:6; 4:15), and some felt a keen, personal loyalty to him. Apollos had come upon the scene later (3:6), rendering a brilliant service in developing the work, and some favored him. (See Acts 18:24-28.) Though there is no evidence that Peter was in Corinth or had visited the city before this letter was written, some leaned toward him as the appointed leader of the Jerusalem apostles. And in a puzzling reference that is nowhere repeated in the letter, others cried out, "I belong to Christ" (1:12). Yet they were guilty of the same factious spirit as the rest.

Scholars have differed greatly in their efforts to explain this reference to the so-called Christ party. Some of the explanations are:

(1) They were spiritualistic Gnostics who recognized no authority except the Spirit of Christ.

(2) They were members of a small rigid group who felt that they were the only real Christians in Corinth.

(3) The comment was Paul's; that is, whereas the Corinthians were naming lesser persons as their leaders, Paul rebutted, "I belong to Christ."

(4) The comment was a copyist's gloss inserted in the margin of the manuscript and later included in the text.

Three Probing Questions (1:13)

In Paul's response to these rival cries, he asked three pointed questions, "Is Christ divided? Was Paul crucified for you? Or were you baptized into the name of Paul?" (v. 13).

All three questions are rhetorical. That is, they did not seek information that Paul did not have. Instead they made strong affirmations by asking dramatic questions that required no answers. In this way Paul sought to shame and shatter all the bombast and misplaced loyalty evidenced in the partisan cries at Corinth.

Each of these questions centered the attention of the Corinthians upon Christ, and there was a good reason for doing so. Factions develop in churches when men take their eyes off Christ and focus them upon men. And factions dissolve when men take their eyes off men and focus them once more upon Christ.

Split churches today cannot improve upon this strategy. If we must have a rallying cry, let it be the basic New Testament confession, "Jesus is Lord" (1 Cor. 12:3).

Priority of Preaching (1:14-17)

In the verses that follow Paul emphasized the fact that he had baptized few of his converts (vv. 14-16). This ministry he entrusted to others, while he devoted his primary energies to the preaching of the gospel. In verse 15 Paul expressed concern lest any convert exaggerate the importance of the role of the baptizer. And in verse 17 he was equally concerned that no one exaggerate the importance of the skills used in the proclamation of the gospel.

Actions which call attention to the preacher himself and cleverness on his part shift the center of wonder from the message to the messenger. They empty the cross of its power.

Message of the Cross (1:18-31)

The emphasis upon the priority of preaching in verse 17 moves naturally to an emphasis upon the message of the cross in verses 18-31. This is one of the greatest passages in the New Testament.

At least three truths about the cross are set forth here.

Necessary to the Knowledge of God (1:18-21)

No man can know God as he most needs to know him apart from the cross. God ever seeks to make himself known to men, and he has several media through which he tries to confront us. Romans 1:20 speaks of God's revelation to us through nature. Romans 2:14-16 describes his revelation through conscience. Romans 3:1-2 refers to his revelation through the Scriptures. But the climax of all God's self-disclosure is in the cross of Jesus Christ, his Son. If we are to know God as we most need to know him, we shall meet him at the cross.

But the world neither likes nor understands this. To it the message of the cross is folly (v. 18). It prefers to discover God through its own wisdom and cleverness. The world has its own spokesman: the wise man, the scribe or professional scholar, and the subtle debater (v. 20). It invokes its own criteria for acceptance or rejection, namely, visible evidence or rational proofs. It has its own prevailing attitude: self-sufficiency and confidence in the power of its own reason and technology.

Yet verse 21 renders a startling indictment of human wisdom as it states that "the world did not know God through wisdom." And this is the fatal flaw in all man's wisdom and ingenuity, both ancient and modern. It leaves him without the knowledge of God.

How scandalous then for a proud and often arrogant race that what it could not achieve through its wisdom, God made available through the cross! Verse 21 reads, "For since, in the wisdom of God, the world did not know God through wisdom, it pleased God through the folly of what we preach to save those who believe."

Requires the Response of Faith (1:22-25)

In verses 22-25 Paul mentioned two groups for whom the call to faith in a crucified Lord was especially offensive. First he pointed to the Jews, who looked for signs that would identify the Messiah who would deliver them from Roman oppression. There was no place in popular Jewish hope for a Messiah who would die on a cross. Thus the summons to faith in Christ constituted a stumblingblock. Second, he pointed to the Greeks, who were enamored with human wisdom and demanded rational proofs. To them the claim that an itinerant Jewish teacher sentenced to die on a Roman cross was the Son of God and Savior of men seemed foolish. Thus the call to faith in him was regarded as utter folly.

However, verse 25 affirms that all who respond in faith to God's call in Jesus Christ experience him as God's power and wisdom—whether Jews or Greeks.

Allows No Boasting in God's Presence (1:26-31)

In verse 26 Paul invited his readers to take a look at those who made up the congregation in Corinth. He observed that very few of their members were among those whom the world esteemed as learned, influential, or socially elite. For these are the categories—brains, clout, and pedigree—which society holds in highest regard. But what about the illiterate, the powerless, and the lowly born? In verses 27-28 Paul made the startling announcement that God had chosen them to become members in his family of grace. It seems that the last place to look for a rerun of the phony distinctions that characterize human society is in God's family.

Yet one needs to be cautious here, else he will attribute to God the opposite side of the world's pattern of pride and prejudice. That is, he will imply that God loves the ignorant, weak, and lowly but rejects the learned, strong, and nobly born. And this would be reverse discrimination, no matter what high-sounding label were attached to it. To exchange prejudices is not to be rid of them.

No! God loves all men regardless of their achievements, positions, or identities. His love does not take its cue from what we are; rather it is an expression of who he is.

Verses 29 and 31 indicate the real reason why not many whom the world regarded as wise, powerful, or well-born were to be found in the church at Corinth. It was because pride tends to characterize those who enjoy such worldly advantages. How can those who have grown accustomed to the adoration of men learn to bend their knees before God? And yet no one can boast in God's presence or strut before him, "Therefore, as it is written, 'Let him who boasts, boast of the Lord' " (v. 31).

But for all those who have answered God's call in Jesus Christ, he has become: (1) our "wisdom," the one through whom we come to know God; (2) our "righteousness," the one who puts us right with God; (3) our "sanctification," the one in whom we are set apart for God; (4) our "redemption," the one who sets us free from the power of sin and death to serve God (v. 30).

Paul's Ministry in Corinth (2:1-5)

The spirit of humility that Paul demanded in his readers, he revealed himself during his visit to Corinth. How did he address the gospel to this great urban center? Our passage affords three basic insights.

First, his *message* was "Jesus Christ and him crucified" (v. 2; see Gal. 3:1). Early Christian proclamation centered in the cross and resurrection of Jesus Christ.

Second, his *manner* was one of fear and trembling (vv. 1,3-4). He did not seek to impress his hearers with displays of oratory or learning. Instead he was fully aware of his own weakness and felt the weight of responsibility that rested upon him as God's messenger. Thus he depended upon the Spirit of God for power.

Third, his *motivation* was the compelling desire that men place their faith in the power of God rather than in the cleverness of men (v. 5).

Churches today seeking to meet the challenge of an increasingly urbanized society cannot improve upon the essential strategy revealed in these verses. So often we do not get New Testament results because we do not embody New Testament commitments.

Christian Wisdom (2:6-16)

This passage shows Paul's leaving his main thought to talk about Christian wisdom. Lest Paul's repudiation of worldly wisdom be misinterpreted as a hostility toward all wisdom, he interrupted his thought long enough to affirm a distinctly Christian concept of wisdom. No attempt at a detailed exposition of the passage will be made here. Instead we will simply note several statements that Paul made about Christian wisdom.

(1) There *is* such a thing as Christian wisdom, and Paul imparted it among the mature (v. 6). Obviously the immaturity of the Corinthians imposed some limitations on what Paul could do for them in this regard.

(2) Christian wisdom is not to be confused with the wisdom of this age, whose rulers, whether human or demonic, failed to understand it (vv. 6,8).

(3) Christian wisdom centers in God's redemptive plan through the ages (vv. 7,9).

(4) Christian wisdom is revealed to us by the Spirit (2:10-12). It does not come by human discovery but by divine disclosure.

(5) Christian wisdom is imparted to others by us who have been taught by the Spirit (v. 13).

(6) Christian wisdom is folly to the unspiritual or natural man (v. 14). He does not receive the things of the Spirit, for they can only be discerned spiritually. But the spiritual man is able to make right judgments (v. 15). He draws upon the unlimited and unfailing Source of all wisdom. He looks at things from the viewpoint of Christ (v. 16).

Carnal Church Members (3:1-23)

In chapter 3 Paul resumed more directly his indictment of the divisions in the church at Corinth. He lamented that he could not address his readers as spiritual men (v. 1). Instead they were carnal men, as evidenced by the jealousy and strife in their midst (v. 3). As mere babes in Christ, they still required a milk diet. Paul could set no solid food before them (v. 2). Their partisan cries were such as one might have expected from unconverted men (v. 4).

In the remaining paragraphs of this chapter Paul sought to overcome the factionalism in Corinth by a powerful mixture of insight, warning, and appeal.

God Gives the Growth (3:5-9)

Two words in verse 5 require special attention: *servants* and *Lord.* How imperative it is that these categories be recognized and respected! God's servants are many, but he alone is Lord. And the roles of servant and Lord must never be confused. Obviously the Corinthians were giving a devotion to some servants of God that rightly belonged only to God.

Paul used an agricultural metaphor to portray the important but subordinate role of man in the work of the gospel. Historically Paul had planted the gospel in Corinth, while Apollos, who came later, watered it. As a result of the faithful labors of both, many were saved. But what was the proper explanation of this harvest? Did Paul or Apollos accomplish their salvation? No! It was *God* who gave the growth (vv. 6-7).

To be sure, there is a oneness of instrumentality in the planting and the watering. Both are required for an abundant harvest. However, it is always possible for one to plant well and another to water poorly, or vice versa. When this happens, the harvest is less, but the faithful worker is not penalized for the faithless performance of his fellow servant. Instead "each shall receive his wages according to his labor" (v. 8). For the basis of God's approval is never the size of the crop but always the intensity of the toil.

This is an encouraging truth for all Christians. It means that every believer has equal access to God's favor. Arduous toil is possible for all God's servants, whereas large crops are not.

Test of Fire (3:10-15)

In these verses Paul reminded the factious Corinthians that God would judge the work of all his servants. Here the metaphor is architectural rather than agricultural as above. Christ was the only foundation that could be laid down, and Paul had done this faithfully in Corinth. Now others were building upon this foundation, and they needed to take care how they were doing it. The adequacy of any building material depends upon the test it will have to meet. For this reason blocks of ice provide suitable housing in the Arctic but would not stand the test of the tropics.

The test that the Christian's building will have to meet is fire on the day of judgment. If he has used combustible materials like wood, hay, or straw, his work will be consumed in the flames. He himself will be saved "but only as through fire" (v. 15). On the other hand, if he has used noncombustible materials like gold, silver, and precious stones, his work will stand the test. He will receive a reward (v. 14).

Surely the reminder of God's impending judgment upon the work of all his servants should give pause to those in Corinth who were responsible for divisions in the church.

Destroying God's Temple (3:16-17)

There was insight but no warning in the agricultural metaphor of verses 5-9. There was sobering but assuring warning in the building metaphor of verses 10-15. But in the temple metaphor of verses 16-17 there is strong warning only. It is one of the severest pronouncements in Paul's writings.

Here the metaphor of the temple is applied to believers. Not the building in which they meet but Christians themselves constitute the temple of God. God's Spirit dwells in them. Certainly those responsible for the factions in Corinth had lost sight of this basic truth and needed to be corrected.

But they needed also to be warned. Nothing destroys a church more completely than dissensions and strife. Thus Paul admonished severely, "If any one destroys God's temple, God will destroy him. For God's temple is holy, and that temple you are" (v. 17).

Folly of Worldly Wisdom (3:18-23)

In the final paragraph of chapter 3 Paul drew a sharp distinction between worldly wisdom and the wisdom of God. What the world regards as wisdom is so offensive to God that Paul urged, "If any one among you thinks that he is wise in this age, let him become a fool that he may become wise. For the wisdom of this world is folly with God" (vv. 18-19).

Paul supported his indictment of worldly wisdom by citing two Old Testament passages: (1) "He catches the wise in their craftiness" (Job 5:13); (2) "The Lord knows that the thoughts of the wise are futile" (Ps.

94:11). The words translated "craftiness" in the first and "thoughts" in the second characterize the wisdom of the world. Together they describe the world's wisdom as cunning and hostile toward God.

Here are men who are crafty in the ways of the world. They know how to maneuver and manipulate to secure their selfish advantage. They do not hesitate to destroy others in order to advance themselves. Measured by the world's standards, they are successful. When these crafty worldlings get into our churches and seek to bring their know-how to the affairs of the kingdom of God, they cause grave calamities. No wonder Paul urged his readers to become fools in the sight of men, that they might become wise in the sight of God.

In verses 21-23 Paul sought to reverse the partisan cries of the Corinthians. They had been boasting of their loyalty to favorite leaders (1:12). Thus they were divided into contending groups or rival factions. Now Paul reminded them of the grand oneness of their inheritance in Jesus Christ.

Personal Defense and Warning (4:1-21)

In chapter 4 Paul brought his discussion of church divisions to an end with a response to those who had questioned his credentials as an apostle (vv. 1-5), an explanation of his purpose in writing as he has written (vv. 6-7), and an attempt to puncture the pride of the Corinthians with some sharp satire (vv. 8-13). His final words expressed apprehension about his forthcoming visit to Corinth (vv. 14-21).

The Servant's Role (4:1-7)

How did Paul want his readers to regard him and other Christian leaders? Keep in mind that he was addressing a church that was divided into partisan groups boasting about their identity with one leader as over against the others. Paul countered this misplaced devotion by instructing the Corinthians to think of their leaders as "servants of Christ and stewards of the mysteries of God" (v. 1). This wisely shifted the focal point of their allegiance away from their leaders to the Lord. Only in this way could the divisions in the church be overcome.

Also, the Corinthians needed to be reminded of the primary qualification of a steward. What was it? Prior associations, the power of spellbinding speech, affability, good looks, or any kind of expertise? No!

Verse 2 instructs, "It is required of stewards that they be found trust-worthy." The reason for this is that stewards deal with that which belongs to another. Thus they have their master's interests at heart and scorn self-serving.

Paul depreciated all human judgment against him (v. 3). But just as fervently he discredited his own self-estimate (v. 4). An unaccusing conscience does not necessarily assure a lack of guilt. It can denote a conscience in need of repair. However, when the Lord returns, he will judge every man (v. 5).

Paul's reason for referring to Apollos and himself in the preceding discussion was to keep the Corinthians from being "puffed up in favor of one against another" (v. 6). They were both servants of Christ, not rival leaders.

Deflation by Satire (4:8-13)

By favoring one leader above another, the Corinthians had assumed the role of judges of apostolic merits. There was an implied claim of superiority in what they were doing. They were acting as though the consummation of the kingdom of God had occurred already and they were basking in its blessed fullness. Thus Paul sought to deflate the proud Corinthians. In a series of barbed exclamations he contrasted their imagined estate with the actual lot of the apostles, whom they presumed to judge. The following arrangement should make this satire more vivid:

Corinthians	Apostles
1. Already you are filled; have become rich; and without us have become kings!	1. God has exhibited us as last of all, like men sentenced to death, a spectacle to all.
2. You are wise in Christ.	2. We are fools for Christ's sake.
3. You are strong.	3. We are weak.
4. You are held in honor.	4. We are held in disrepute, treated as the scum of the earth.

Personal Appeal (4:14-21)

In writing to the Corinthians in this way, Paul explained that he was exercising the right of a father to counsel his children (vv. 14-15). To remind them further of his ways in Christ, he was sending Timothy to them (v. 17). And later he himself would come and deal with the arrogant ones. He would come with a rod of correction, if necessary, but he preferred to come "with love in a spirit of gentleness" (v. 21).

Moral Issues
5:1 to 6:20

Rivalries and factions were not the only evidences of worldly intrusion in the church at Corinth. There was also a casual attitude toward sexual immorality. This may have derived from a gnostic distortion of the gospel which affirmed unconditional moral freedom. If so, it was not the last time that sophisticated men have misinterpreted the gospel of grace to justify an ethic of license. Or it may have reflected the difficulty of planting a Christian conscience regarding sexual relationships in a society that was notoriously immoral.

At any rate, the pressures to conform to an immoral society were strong in the church at Corinth, even as they are in our own day. Thus we are not surprised to learn that Paul devoted the next two chapters of 1 Corinthians to a discussion of moral issues. In chapter 5 he rebuked the church for tolerating an instance of flagrant immorality in its midst. In chapter 6 he reproved his readers for their readiness to sue one another in pagan courts (vv. 1-11) and to engage in sexual intercourse with prostitutes (vv. 12-20).

Immorality in the Church (5:1-13)

Shocking Permissiveness (5:1-2)

Word of the flagrant case of sexual sin had reached Paul, and he was deeply distressed by it. The problem involved a man in the church who was living in an illicit sexual relationship with his stepmother—the most probable meaning of the phrase "his father's wife." Evidently she was a pagan, for Paul did not include her in his instructions. Whether she was widowed or divorced was not indicated, and no mention was made of her husband.

This moral wrong took on extra dimensions of shame, because both father and son had engaged in sexual relationships with the same woman. The Old Testament expressly forbade this in Leviticus 18:7-8; 20:11. Likewise Roman law prohibited such unions, even after the death of the father, as evidenced in the Institutes of Gaius. It is not that sexual relationships of this sort never occurred in ancient pagan society, but that they were generally condemned.

What was the church's attitude toward this evil? Those reporting the matter to Paul stated that the people still were puffed up with pride (v. 2). The same arrogance that had blinded them in their factions to the oneness of Christ (1:10 to 4:21) had also rendered them insensitive to the moral outrage in their midst.

Once again the sinful world order had invaded the church at Corinth. This time the breakthrough had occurred in the vital sector of sexual morality. At stake was the integrity of the Christian witness to an immoral society, but the smug Corinthians were too carnal to recognize that the breach had taken place. Paul chided them for their failure to mourn and to take action against the offending member (v. 2).

Exclusion Demanded (5:3-5)

Though in Ephesus when apprised of the deplorable state of affairs in Corinth (16:8), Paul did not allow his absence to absolve him of responsibility. He was absent in body only. In spirit he was present, and he had already pronounced judgment upon the man (v. 3). He instructed the whole church to assemble to deal with the problem. This obligation was neither relegated to the pastoral leadership nor to a committee. It concerned all and needed the weight of the entire congregation behind it.

As a gathered community of faith, they were to meet in the name of Jesus Christ and with his power. Then under these solemn circumstances Paul ordered the church, "You are to deliver this man to Satan for the destruction of the flesh, that his spirit may be saved in the day of the Lord Jesus" (v. 5). Observe the following:

(1) The form of discipline applied here was exclusion from the church. It was suggested first in verse 2.

(2) Apparently the world outside the church was regarded as Satan's domain.

(3) The purpose of the action was redemptive. It was not merely punitive. Rather it sought the destruction of the sinful nature; that is, the flesh, which had gained the upper hand in the man's moral collapse. The end hoped for was the salvation of the man in the final judgment.

There is a great principle here. Discipline in the New Testament is primarily restorative or redemptive. It seeks the reclamation of the member in the wrong.

Evil As Leaven (5:6-8)

To appreciate Paul's message in these verses, one needs to study the Old Testament passages relating to the observance of the Passover and the Feast of Unleavened Bread. The basic material is found in Exodus 12:1-51; Leviticus 23:4-8; and Deuteronomy 16:1-8.

According to Exodus 12:8 unleavened bread was eaten with the roasted lamb and bitter herbs during the original Passover meal in Egypt. Simply made and quickly eaten, it was especially suitable for quick escape. Severe judgment fell upon any Israelite who ate leavened bread during this time (Ex. 12:15). Thus great care was exercised in Jewish homes to search out and dispose of the old leaven. Wives examined cracks in kneading boards, lest an undiscovered bit of fermented dough should become dislodged and contaminate the new batch.

With these concepts in the background, Paul rebuked the Corinthians for their complacency regarding the immoral member. He likened the presence of the immoral person in the church to old leaven that would contaminate the whole batch (v. 6). Thus he called for the cleansing out of the old leaven (v. 7). Christ, our paschal lamb, has been sacrificed, and the call given to celebrate the festival "with the unleavened bread of sincerity and truth" (v. 8).

Here we derive another principle of church discipline in the New Testament: it was realistic about the contagion of evil. Tolerated evil is exceedingly pervasive. When immorality is condoned in a church, the moral fiber of the entire church is weakened. None escape its contamination, including the leadership. The *whole* lump is leavened.

Observe that the call to celebration in verse 8 is contingent upon the demand for cleansing in verse 7. No church can celebrate the deliverance from sin that Christ makes possible while sheltering sin in its members.

Previous Letter Clarified (5:9-13)

At this point Paul found it necessary to clear up a misunderstanding of the letter he had sent earlier to Corinth. (See Introduction.) Actually he had urged his readers not to continue in fellowship with immoral church members (5:11). However, they had understood him to say that they must withdraw from associations with all immoral persons in the world (5:10). Paul corrected their misunderstanding, affirming that it was God's responsibility to judge those outside the church (5:13). However, the church does carry the responsibility of self-judgment (v. 12).

The problem in Corinth was not that the church was living in the midst of an immoral society. That is exactly where the Lord intended her to be. Rather it was the low estimate of what it meant to be the people of God in the world. This had permitted the immoral society to invade the church. Thus for the fourth time in a brief chapter of thirteen verses, Paul demanded the exclusion of the immoral church member, "Drive out the wicked person from among you" (5:13; see also vv. 2,5,7).

Lawsuits in Pagan Courts (6:1-11)

The Problem (6:1-4)

In chapters 1—4 Paul dealt with the problem of church factions. Instead of functioning as the body of Christ, the church was divided into rival groups, issuing challenges to one another. Now in this passage Paul turned his attention to personal disputes among church members. Evidently some were contending about personal rights or business matters. Unable to resolve their differences, they sought redress in pagan courts of law.

Paul was distressed at two points. First, how ludicrous it was for those destined to participate in the final judgment to show themselves "incompetent to try trivial cases" (v. 2)! Surely those being prepared to deal with the issues of the ages ought not to reveal an inability to resolve the problems of the moment (v. 3).

Second, Paul thought it particularly tragic for believers to carry their disputes before pagan judges. This was to discredit the gospel in the eyes of the pagan society to which the church was commissioned to bear witness. It misrepresented the emphasis on love that lay at the heart of the Christian message. It confessed to the world that the trifling disputes that shattered its fellowship were greater than their common bond in Christ.

Paul did not intend to depreciate the courts, or to imply that all pagan judges were corrupt and incapable of administering justice. Instead he was concerned because the quarreling Corinthians were depreciating the gospel by their readiness to sue one another.

Alternatives to Litigation (6:5-8)

Arbitration within the church (6:5-6).—"Can it be that there is no man among you wise enough to decide between members of the brotherhood?" (v. 5). The Corinthians had boasted of their wisdom. Surely, then, it was not necessary to go outside their congregation to find one competent to render a judgment in their disputes.

Jews enjoyed a large measure of autonomy in the ancient world. Disputes that arose within the Jewish communities were settled among themselves. Indeed, the rabbis taught that it was unlawful for a Jew to seek a judge's decision in pagan courts.

Moreover, in the pagan world there were religious brotherhoods and mutual benefit societies who pledged not to sue one another in the courts. Instead the disputes were settled through arbitration within the group. No wonder then that Paul was distressed that "brother goes to law against brother, and that before unbelievers" (v. 6).

Enduring the wrong (6:7-8).—It was lamentable that serious disputes should arise among Christians. Such breakdowns in relationships needed to be recognized as an utter defeat for all. Once in process, however, it would have been better for the dispute to be resolved fairly within the church family. But rather than discrediting the gospel by seeking redress in pagan courts, Paul advised his readers to endure the wrong (v. 7). Instead they were using the courts in attempts to defraud one another (v. 8).

Relation to the Kingdom of God (6:9-11)

In the preceding verses Paul had discussed a particular form of unrighteous conduct, namely, the readiness to sue or defraud one another in court. Now he broadened his discussion to include other forms of unrighteousness. By this association he underscored the wrong of cheating others, and he prepared the way for the refutation of sexual immorality in the next paragraph (vv. 12-20). Thus verses 9-11 are both climactic and transitional.

Twice in these verses Paul affirmed that the unrighteous have no inheritance in God's kingdom (vv. 9-10). The warning is timely, for men easily persuade themselves that God will not hold them responsible for their sins. They confuse indulgence, in which one continues to sin and imagines that God ever pardons, with forgiveness, which always demands repentance.

Sexual Immorality (6:12-20)

Here we have the most important passage in Paul's letters on the subject of sexual immorality. In a relatively brief paragraph of a pastoral letter, he challenged the casual attitude toward sexual wrong that prevailed in Corinth, and he stated several aspects of the Christian case for sexual purity.

Refutation of Popular Slogans (6:12-14)

One of these slogans is repeated twice in verse 12, "All things are lawful for me." And the other is stated in verse 13, "Food is meant for the stomach and the stomach for food." These verses need to be read in a modern translation that sets off the slogans in quotation marks, or one may find himself attributing to Paul the very teachings he was seeking to refute.

What was the background of these slogans used by the Corinthian libertines to rationalize complete freedom in sexual indulgence? Some have suggested a distortion of Paul's teaching about the Christian's freedom from observing the Levitical code of clean and unclean foods. The libertines thus may have claimed that sexual morality was no more important than the distinctions between foods.

An increasing number of scholars, however, find in the passage evidence of a gnosticizing tendency in the church at Corinth. This tendency was manifested in a dualism that distinguished sharply between soul and body. The former alone was good, whereas the latter was inherently evil. Those identified with this tendency regarded themselves as the spiritual ones. They affirmed a complete salvation, one in which they were freed from the flesh. They claimed an unconditional moral freedom, denying the consequences of sin.

In either instance sexual immorality was being rationalized as allowable or irrelevant. Satisfying sexual hunger was no more wrong than eating a bowl of stew. Both were fulfillments of bodily hungers, and neither had any meaning for the essential self.

Paul challenged the moral looseness epitomized in the slogans in two ways. First, he qualified the statement regarding Christian freedom, " 'All things are lawful for me,' but not all things are helpful. 'All things are lawful for me,' but I will not be enslaved by anything" (v. 12). Thus Paul insisted that the Christian exercise his freedom in a thoroughly responsible way. Otherwise his freedom would become license. Any claim of Christian liberty that leads to futility or enslavement is a contradiction.

Second, Paul affirmed the importance of the body, "The body was not meant for immorality, but for the Lord, and the Lord for the body" (v. 13). Thus he confronted the libertines who excused their sexual sins by declaring that the body had no significance. And in verse 14 Paul climaxed his insistence upon the importance of the body by pointing ahead to the resurrection.

Intercourse with Prostitutes (6:15-16)

For many in Corinth, sexual relations with a cult prostitute had a religious significance. It signified consecration to the cult goddess.

For sailors visiting Corinth after sea duty, the favors of a prostitute did not always have such a religious connotation. Rather it was a feature of the debauchery commonly associated with shore leave.

For libertines with gnostic tendencies in Corinth, intercourse with a prostitute was neither regarded as an act of consecration nor debauchery. It was simply the satisfaction of an appetite of a body that was destined to be destroyed by God. No moral issue was at stake, they affirmed, for the truly enlightened or liberated person.

But for Christians Paul insisted that intercourse with a prostitute was a terrible desecration of the body. Our bodies are members of Christ. So complete is the believer's identification with Christ that when he commits fornication with a prostitute, he involves Christ in his act (vv. 15-16). No wonder that Paul expressed such revulsion at the thought!

Flee Sexual Immorality (6:18-20)

The word translated "shun" is literally *flee.* It is a vigorous metaphor that Paul used only twice in the entire letter. He used it in 1 Corinthians 10:14 with regard to idolatry and here in connection with sexual immorality. Both of these forms of degradation have an affinity for each other. And Paul's counsel regarding both was to flee from them, to seek safety in flight.

Some people fail morally because they insist on spending time where temptation abounds. Yet in sexual temptation one does well neither to underestimate its power nor to overestimate one's strength to refuse.

In verses 18-20 Paul supported his command to flee from sexual immorality with the following reasons:

(1) *It has a tragic uniqueness as a sin against the body (v. 18).* To be sure, there are other sins against the body (gluttony, drunkenness, and drug addiction). But none involves so complete a giving of the total person in a way that opposes the will of God.

(2) *It desecrates the body, which is the temple of the Holy Spirit (v. 19).* At conversion the Holy Spirit comes to dwell in the life of the believer. Thus in a wondrous sense the body of the Christian becomes a temple of the Holy Spirit. For this reason sexual immorality is an act of desecration. It profanes the Spirit's temple.

(3) *It ignores the costliness of our redemption (vv. 19-20).* One says, "I am my own man," affirming his independence. And this aptly describes the life of the unconverted. But the Christian is not his own man. He has been bought with a price, and Christ is Lord in his life by virtue of the costly redemption he has achieved. (See 1 Pet. 1:17-19; Eph. 1:7.)

(4) *It fails to glorify God in the body (v. 20).* The body is a medium through which the Christian may glorify God. (See Phil. 1:20-21.) When the body is regarded in this way, it requires the highest level of Christian integrity in sexual relationships.

Marriage and Divorce
7:1-40

In chapter 7 we reach a turning point in the letter. It begins, "Now concerning the matters about which you wrote" (7:1). This introductory formula indicates that from this point on Paul was largely responding to questions that the Corinthians themselves had raised in a letter. The subjects inquired about were marriage and divorce (7:1-40), eating food offered to idols (8:1 to 11:1), charismatic gifts (12:1 to 14:40), the relief offering for Jerusalem (16:1-4), and the plans of Apollos (16:12).

In chapter 7 Paul dealt with some of the problems of Christian marriage in a pagan city. As the gospel had been preached in Corinth, sometimes both a husband and wife became Christians. What implications did their new commitment have for them in their relationships to each other? In other instances only the husband or the wife became a believer, leaving a mixed marriage. Should a Christian continue to share life's most intimate union with a pagan partner? Others who heard the gospel and believed were unmarried or widows. Should they marry or remarry? There is even the possibility that some in Corinth were advocating spiritual or celibate marriages, that is, marriages in which a couple lived together without sexual relations. What does being a Christian have to say about such matters?

In answering these questions, Paul appealed wherever possible to the recorded teaching of Jesus (v. 10). But in some instances the Corinthians had raised questions for which no appeal could be made to Jesus' teachings (vv. 12,25). After all, the religious and cultural settings of Capernaum and Corinth were not the same. In such cases Paul had to give his own opinion "as one who by the Lord's mercy is trustworthy" (v. 25).

Where Both Husband and Wife Are Christians (7:1-7,10-11).

Paul's preference for celibacy (7:1-2,7).—Many would like to rescue Paul from his apparent depreciation of marriage in this chapter. For example, some suggest that verse 1 was not Paul's statement. Rather it expressed the view of the spiritualists or ascetics in Corinth who taught that Christians should not marry at all. To them Paul gave the practical counsel in verse 2 that marriage would provide protection against the ever present sexual temptations in Corinth.

But this seems a strained reading of the text. Throughout the chapter there are other verses in which Paul's preference for the single status is repeated (vv. 7-8,38,40). Indeed, in verse 7 Paul implied that his celibacy was a charismatic gift. It equipped him to fulfill his itinerant ministry as an apostle without undue distraction from sexual temptation. Thus the gift *(charisma)* fitted the calling. And in the same verse Paul acknowledged that not all have the gift of celibacy.

A sexual partnership (7:3-6).—If marriage is to provide a security against sexual temptation, both husband and wife must seek to become the most adequate sexual partner possible. "For the wife does not rule over her own body, but the husband does; likewise the husband does not rule over his own body, but the wife does" (v. 4). Thus neither is to refuse sexual relations to the other except under the circumstances spelled out in verse 5: (1) by common consent, since it is a decision that involves both; (2) for a limited time, not indefinitely; (3) for a special season of prayer. Then the normal pattern of conjugal relations are to be resumed, "lest Satan tempt you through lack of self-control" (v. 5).

From these few verses we learn some important features of the Christian concept of marriage:

(1) It is a monogamous relationship: one husband and one wife for life.

(2) No premarital or extramarital sex is permitted.

(3) Sex contributes to the fulfillment of the marriage relationship, and is not limited to having children.

(4) Everything demanded of a wife as an adequate sexual companion is likewise demanded of the husband. The principle of mutuality prevails.

Sanctity of marriage (7:10-11).—Here Paul made a direct appeal to the teachings of Jesus. Obviously in the report of Jesus' teachings to which he had access, no grounds for divorce were mentioned. A husband and wife should not separate. If they do, let them either remain single or be reconciled to each other.

There is no hint here of the so-called exceptive clause found in Matthew 5:32 and 19:9, "except for unchastity."

Where Only One Is a Christian (7:12-24)

Evidently the Corinthians had asked Paul whether or not a believer should continue to live in marriage with a pagan. In his response he acknowledged that he could not appeal to the reported teachings of Jesus for an answer. Thus he would have to give his own opinion. And in his answer he emphasized two principles.

Initiative belongs to the unbeliever (7:12-16).—If the unbelieving wife or husband wants the marriage to continue, then the Christian partner is to continue in the marriage. Verse 14 is intended to support the instruction given in verses 12-13, but its meaning is far from obvious. Certainly Paul was not teaching the salvation of a pagan by marriage to a Christian as an alternative to faith in Christ. Nevertheless the marriage of a Christian and a pagan had a quality not to be found in the marriage of two pagans. Somehow and in some sense, through the intimate association of marriage to a believer, the unbeliever was consecrated. And thus their children were holy. A benefit is described, though its precise nature and extent are not defined.

On the other hand, if the unbelieving partner desires to separate, the

Christian should permit the marriage to dissolve peaceably (v. 15). Again, verse 16 is intended to support the counsel of verse 15, but its sense is obscure. Thus the Revised Standard Version translates it, "Wife, how do you know whether you will save your husband? Husband, how do you know whether you will save your wife?" But *The New English Bible* yields a different meaning, "Think of it: as a wife you may be your husband's salvation; as a husband you may be your wife's salvation."

"God has called us to peace" (7:17-24).—This statement in verse 15 supported Paul's instruction to the Christian not to oppose the pagan companion's determination to end the marriage. Christian husbands and wives cannot win their unsaved mates to the Lord by making them angry.

Verses 17-24 provide an elaboration upon the emphasis made in verse 15 on the call of God as a call to peace. Paul applied the principle to circumcision and slavery, and summed up his instruction in verse 24, "So, brethren, in whatever state each was called, there let him remain with God."

Counsel for the Unmarried and Widows (7:8-9,25-40)

Throughout this lengthy passage, Paul repeated his earlier assessment of singleness as a more desirable state than marriage. Marriage was allowable but singleness was preferable. And the reasons given for the former seemed less impressive than those given for the latter.

Observe several tensions in the passage.

The moral tension (7:8-9).—Paul advised the unmarried and widows to remain single as he was. "But if they cannot exercise self-control, they should marry. For it is better to marry than to be aflame with passion" (7:9).

Paul's statement affirmed marriage as the desirable alternative to sexual temptation. Though true, this is not the loftiest motivation for marriage. The teachings of Jesus on marriage in Mark 10:6-9, for example, sound a higher note.

Furthermore, Paul's statement was true relatively rather than absolutely. The assumption suggests that if one marries, he will no longer have to contend with sexual temptation. But married people know that struggles with sexual temptation continue beyond the marriage altar. Even so, Christian marriage is a powerful contributor to sexual morality.

The eschatological tension (7:25-31).—Paul believed that he was living in the tumultuous times that would precede the end of the world. Three times in this brief paragraph he underscored this conviction, and it bore directly upon his advice regarding marriage. In verse 26 he wrote, "I think that in view of the present distress it is well for a person to remain as he is." Thus if one is married, he should not seek to be free, and if one is unmarried, he should not seek a mate (7:27). Yet if one does marry, he does not sin (7:28).

Similar statements may be found in verses 29 and 31.

The domestic tension (7:32-35).—Paul felt that it was better to remain single, in order to avoid the distractions of marriage. In verses 32 and 34 he presented a rather idealistic view of the unmarried man and woman respectively. Both devoted their full energies to the Lord's work, striving to please him. On the other hand, the married were portrayed as having divided interests. They were anxious about worldly affairs and how to please their companions (7:33-34). Paul insisted that his purpose was not to burden his readers with needless restraint "but to promote good order and to secure your undivided devotion to the Lord" (7:35).

Once again, the point that Paul made was true relatively rather than absolutely. The Christian man or woman who has no family responsibilities is free to devote more time and energy to the Lord's work. Not all of them do. Furthermore, not all Christian couples fit the pattern of worldly distraction described in these verses. In Romans 16:3-5 Paul commended Priscilla and Aquila as his fellow workers in Christ, who had risked their necks to save his life.

An unresolved problem in translation (7:36-38).—Because of uncertainties regarding the meaning of some words in these verses, we cannot be sure whom Paul was addressing. Nor can we know definitely the details of his instruction. This accounts for the large differences in translation.

For example, the Revised Standard Version translates this instruction as if it were addressed to men who were having problems containing their sexual desires toward their betrothed. Paul stated that it was no sin for them to marry. However, those who were able to control their desires and refrain from marriage chose the better course.

The King James Version translates this instruction as if it were addressed to fathers or guardians of single girls who were approaching the critical point of their marriageable years. Paul stated that it was no sin for them to make marriage arrangements for their daughters. However, those who determined not to give their daughters in marriage did better.

And *The New English Bible* translates this passage as if it were addressed to Christian husbands who were having problems refraining from sexual intercourse with their wives, their partners in celibacy. In these so-called spiritual marriages the husband and wife lived together without sexual relations. Paul stated that it was no sin for these husbands to consummate their marriages. Of course, had they been able to preserve their partners in their virginity, they would have done better.

Remarriage for widows (7:39-40).—Paul stated that a wife was bound to her husband as long as he lived. However, if he died, she was free to marry another man "in the Lord" (v. 39). However, Paul thought that she would be happier if she remained a widow. "And I think that I have the Spirit of God" (v. 40).

Relating to a Pagan Society
8:1 to 11:1

No Christian reading these pages lost any sleep last night over whether or not he should eat food that has been offered to idols. Nor has any wrestled with the decision as to whether or not he should accept an invitation to a cultic meal in a pagan temple. To be sure, Christians in Corinth had to resolve such matters, but they seem remote to us. Thus the reader may conclude too readily that 1 Corinthians 8:1 to 11:1 has historical value only, and does not address life where he lives it.

However, nothing could be farther from the truth, for Christians of every time and culture face the many difficulties of relating to a pagan society. Though the specific issues may vary from one historical period to another, the basic problem remains the same: How can we serve as the people of God in the midst of a pagan environment?

The problem has two facets for the believer. Not only does he live out his pilgrimage of faith as an individual but also as a member of a congregation. And within the body of believers there are members of differing levels of maturity. Those recently saved out of paganism will require special consideration as they begin to grow spiritually. This can prove irksome to the more mature members.

It did in Corinth. Let's look at the situation more closely and see how Paul dealt with it.

Eating Food Offered to Idols (8:1-13)

The Issue (8:1-3)

There were pagan temples in Corinth where animal sacrifices were offered to the gods. Only limited portions of the animal were used, leaving the greater part to be consumed by the priests and worshipers in a cultic meal. Following the sacrifices, the magistrates sold to the butcher shops nearby whatever meat remained. This was the best meat available. Anyone having a dinner party in his home would be sure to serve it to his guests.

What was the Christian's responsibility in this setting? If invited to participate in a cultic meal at a pagan temple, should he go? Was he permitted to buy meat in the local markets that had been consecrated in pagan worship? If invited to the home of a pagan friend for dinner, was he free to accept?

A sharp difference of opinion regarding the answers to these questions divided the church in Corinth. Some, boasting of the knowledge they possessed, felt that they could do all of these things without harm. Paul was not disposed to dispute the claim. However, the attitude that it reflected made him uneasy. Thus he reminded them, " 'Knowledge' puffs up, but love builds up" (v. 1). He knew that one could tear up the fellowship of a congregation if knowledge were the only criterion invoked as a guide to right conduct. Knowledge, untempered by other qualities, fosters pride and arrogance. But love never does. Instead it edifies or builds up the church.

Knowledge of the Mature (8:4-6)

At first, Paul took his stand with the more mature members of the church. He shared their knowledge that " 'an idol has no real existence' " and that " 'there is no God but one' " (v. 4). To be sure, there was no shortage of so-called gods in the ancient world. Their images and shrines abounded on every hand. However, Paul denied any real existence to an idol. In verse 6 he affirmed his faith, "Yet for us there is one God, the Father, from whom are all things and for whom we exist, and one Lord Jesus Christ, through whom are all things and through whom we exist." This expression of faith may have been an early Christian confession.

What bearing did this discussion have upon the problem of eating food offered to idols? The answer is obvious. Since an idol represents something that does not exist, meat consecrated to it could not profane anyone. It remained simply meat neither more nor less. This meant that the mature Christian could buy and eat it with no defilement whatever. Christian liberty rendered meaningless all such superstitions.

Limitations of the Immature (8:7-12)

However, Paul reminded his mature readers that not all in the church had this level of understanding. "But some, through being hitherto accustomed to idols, eat food as really offered to an idol; and their conscience, being weak, is defiled" (v. 7). Verse 8 suggests that some of the mature may have been flaunting their freedom to eat such food, supposing that God esteemed them more highly for doing so. They may have argued that those who had scruples about such things should be shocked into maturity. But Paul quickly repudiated any such tendency.

Instead he admonished the enlightened not to permit their liberty to become a stumbling-block to the immature (v. 9). This could happen if the weak saw them eating in an idol's temple, and attempted to follow their example (v. 10). The resulting disaster to the conscience of the weak was a sin against Christ (vv. 11-12).

Love's Requirement (8:13)

What then does love require? Paul summed up the great principle of voluntary self-limitation for the sake of others in a well-known statement, "Therefore, if food is a cause of my brother's falling, I will never eat meat, lest I cause my brother to fall" (v. 13).

Paul's Example (9:1-27)

Throughout the preceding chapter Paul had urged his more mature readers to exercise their Christian freedom in a responsible way. They were not to insist upon personal rights that would prove to be harmful to the spiritually immature. To do so would be to abandon love as the guiding principle in Christian conduct. Instead they should forego such liberties out of a larger concern for their brother's welfare.

Of course, anyone advocating lofty ethical principles had better be prepared for an intensive scrutiny of his own life. Paul was conscious of this (v. 3). For this reason he devoted an entire chapter to a personal account of his efforts to live on the high level he recommended to others. He indicated four areas in which concern for others led him to renounce or limit his rights or liberties: (1) marriage (v. 5); (2) financial support (vv. 4,6-18); (3) cultural bias (vv. 19-23); (4) self-discipline (vv. 24-27).

Marriage (9:5)

Paul wrote, "Do we not have a right to be accompanied by a wife, as the other apostles and the brothers of the Lord and Cephas?" (v. 5). The question was rhetorical; that is, it did not seek information that Paul lacked. Actually it was an emphatic way of claiming that he did have a right to marry a Christian woman. But he yielded it out of a consideration for his ministry to others. (See 1 Cor. 7:7, where he attributed his capacity to live a celibate life to a charismatic gift.)

Financial Support (9:4,6-18)

Paul seemed especially sensitive about the issue of financial support in his relations with the church in Corinth. Apparently some there stood ready to impugn his motives if he accepted it.

Observe the several evidences that Paul advanced to establish his right to receive financial support as a minister of the gospel: (1) *He drew upon examples from everyday life (v. 7).* The soldier does not serve at his own expense; the one who plants a vineyard eats some of its fruit; and the one who tends a flock is entitled to some of the milk. (2) *He appealed to the Scripture (vv. 8-12).* Paul cited Deuteronomy 25:4, a verse located in the midst of instructions limiting judicial flogging (25:1-3) and the law of levirate marriage (25:5-10). Nothing in the original context suggests ministerial support. Instead the law demanded that an ox should be permitted to eat an occasional mouthful of the grain it was helping to thresh. Nevertheless Paul found here scriptural evidence for the right of ministerial support. (3) *He pointed to the prevailing custom in the Temple service (v. 13).* Those who served at the altar shared in the sacrificial offerings. Numbers 18:8-32 and Deuteronomy 18:1-8 describe this custom among the Jews. (4) *He appealed to the teachings of Jesus.* "In the same way, the Lord commanded that those who proclaim the gospel should get their living by the gospel" (v. 14; see Matt. 10:9-10; Luke 10:7).

What a strong case for ministerial support! One might have expected at this point that Paul would ask the Corinthians to make a sizable contribution to support his missionary labors in Ephesus and beyond. But no! He promptly declared, "Nevertheless, we have not made use of this right, but we endure anything rather than put an obstacle in the way of the gospel of Christ" (v. 12). Nor did he have any intention of seeking financial help from them in the future (v. 15). A divine commision, not a monetary attraction, was the motivation for his preaching. In fact, Paul found his reward in preaching the gospel without any thought of compensation, "not making full use of my right in the gospel" (v. 18).

Cultural Bias (9:19-23)

Just think of all the varied circumstances in which Paul was able to witness effectively. In Antioch of Pisidia he used a synagogue of the Jewish Dispersion to proclaim the gospel (see Acts 13:14-52). In Lystra, a city of Lycaonia, he addressed an excited pagan crowd in the open air (see Acts 14:8-18). In Athens, the cultural center of Greece, he spoke boldly to those who were well-grounded in ancient and contemporary philosophies (see Acts 17:16-34). In Jerusalem he secured permission from the Roman tribune to make his defense to the Jewish mob that had sought to assassinate him (see Acts 22:1-21). In the great audience hall at Caesarea he related his experience with Jesus Christ before the imposing company of the Roman procurator Festus, King Agrippa and Bernice, the military tribunes, and prominent civic leaders (see Acts 25:23 to 26:32). The Colossian letter reveals his capacity to take the terms of an eclectic philosophy that threatened the gospel and make them subservient to it.

No one in the early churches had a wider range of effective witness than Paul. This was possible because of his dedicated flexibility. He was willing to take the risks involved in moving beyond his cultural base. He had unusual skill in distinguishing between the essential and nonessential in the proclamation of the gospel. He was willing to adapt to the cultural bias of his listeners, in order to share Jesus Christ with as many as possible. And he did it without compromising the gospel.

It costs to do this, for there is security in cultural rigidity. It has all the time-honored traditions, all the familiar structures, all the well-traveled paths, and all the well-honed phrases. There is a minimum of risk-taking or surprise if one never moves far from his cultural base, or takes it with him wherever he goes.

A problem arises, however, when men equate their cultural rigidity with orthodoxy. To them Paul's efforts to "become all things to all men" that he might win some (9:22) are compromising the faith. But no! Compromise does not know where to *stand,* and rigidity does not know where to *bend.* Paul did.

Self-Discipline (9:24-27)

At this point Paul turned his attention away from limitations self-imposed out of a consideration for others. Now he looked within to the struggle with bodily appetites, which is common to the lives of all Christians. He, too, confronted the necessity of maintaining control over desires that register a constant protest against restraints of any kind.

For illustrations of the Christian's need for self-discipline, Paul used vigorous athletic metaphors. Since the Isthmian games were held in Corinth every two years, these illustrations were popular and communicated well to most of his readers.

The athlete submitted to strict training routines as he prepared to participate in the games. But all the self-control demanded for peak performance was not too great a price to pay, if the runner won the race and received the victor's wreath (v. 25). Look what the athlete will do to win a wreath that eventually withers away. Ought not the Christian to train even harder for a victor's wreath that is imperishable?

With the Greek boxer in mind, Paul insisted that he did not flail the air with his punches. He was no shadowboxer (v. 26). Instead he dealt a decisive blow to his body, whose appetites clamored to take charge (v. 27). Actually the word translated *pommel* means to "strike under the eye," to deliver a knockout blow.

Why did Paul deal so rigorously with his bodily appetites? He explained it in verse 27, "I pommel my body and subdue it, lest after preaching to others I myself should be disqualified."

Warning Against Presumption (10:1 to 11:1)

How close to idolatry can you get without being an idolater? By their actions, the self-designated elite of the church in Corinth seemed to be exploring this question. They regarded themselves as the truly spiritual members of the congregation, claiming to base their actions on superior insights (v. 1). They advocated freedom with no restraints as the essential expression of their enlightenment, and this freedom included the right to participate in cultic meals at pagan temples (v. 10; 10:14-22).

Apparently this right was based upon the false assumption that Christian baptism and participation in the Lord's Supper made them immune to any harmful consequences from idolatrous practices. The cultural background of the Corinthians provided a conditioning for attaching magical powers to similar religious rites.

Thus Paul pointed to the disastrous experiences of Israel following the Exodus from Egypt to jolt them out of their complacency and arrogance. *Faith in God* must never become *presumption upon God.*

Israel's Folly (10:1-5)

The Christians in Corinth had experienced baptism and the Lord's Supper and thus felt that their standing with God was unalterably secured. So what then, if they chose to participate in cultic meals in pagan temples? No harm could come to them.

Paul sought to refute their false assurance by referring to corresponding experiences in the life of ancient Israel. In verses 1-2 he described Israel's baptism, "I want you to know, brethren, that our fathers were all under the cloud, and all passed through the sea, and all were baptized into Moses in the cloud and in the sea." In verses 3-4 he showed how Israel had also participated in meals provided supernaturally by God, "All ate the same supernatural food and all drank the same supernatural drink." To Paul they were analogous to the Lord's Supper shared by Christians.

Yet the Israelites' "baptism" and "Lord's Supper" did not guarantee their entrance into the Promised Land. They did not continue in faith and obedience, but rather lapsed into such sins as were enumerated in verses 6-10. Thus it was not as though they had continued in faith and obedience, "And yet, most of them were not accepted by God, for the desert was strewn with their corpses" (v. 5, NEB).

Think of it! All these men and women had experienced God's deliverance from Egypt and participated in the meals God provided miraculously in the wilderness. Yet their bones bleached under a desert sun, while God waited for a whole generation to die before resuming his redemptive plan to establish his people in Canaan.

For Our Admonition (10:6-13)

If self-trust and self-will had such dire consequences for the people of God in the time of Moses, certainly they should be avoided in Paul's day—and ours. Thus Paul stated in verse 6 that "these things are warnings for us." In verses 6-10 he listed five examples of the sins of the Israelites that led to their downfall. The Corinthians, who were succumbing to the allurements of their pagan environment, needed to pay particular attention. The five sins were: (1) *desiring evil* (v. 6; see Num. 11:4-34); (2) *worshiping idols* (v. 7; see Ex. 32:1-6); (3) *sexual immorality* (v. 8; see Num. 25:1-9); (4) *putting the Lord to the test* (v. 9; see Num. 21:4-9); (5) *grumbling* (v. 10; see Num. 16:1-50).

In these experiences of Israel, Paul found warnings for his own day, which he believed was moving rapidly toward the end of the age (v. 11). Presumption upon God has always brought disaster: "Therefore let anyone who stands take heed lest he fall" (v. 12). However, God will not permit us to be tempted beyond our strength. With the temptation he will also provide the way to escape (v. 13).

Flee Idolatry (10:14-22)

With regard to the sins of sexual immorality and idolatry, Paul's urgent counsel was to flee, to seek safety in flight (v. 14; see 6:18). He supported his command by describing the believer's experience in the observance of the Lord's Supper. Partaking of the elements involved participation in the blood and body of Christ (v. 16). He appealed also to the meaning of the Jewish sacrifices. Those who ate the sacrifices were partners in the altar (v. 18).

Paul did not refute what he had said earlier about the nothingness of idols and the food offered to them (v. 19; see 8:4-6). Nevertheless he insisted "that what pagans sacrifice they offer to demons and not to God" (v. 20). Though the idols represent gods that do not exist, the worship of them involves the worship of demons. How then can one who has participated with Christ in the Lord's Supper also commune with demons in a pagan cultic meal (v. 21)? To attempt to do so is to provoke the Lord to jealousy (v. 22; see Deut. 32:21) and to invite the same judgment that fell on idolatrous Israel in the wilderness.

Specific Instructions (10:23 to 11:1)

Paul urged his readers to eat whatever meat was sold in the market. They were not to make an issue as to whether or not it had been offered in pagan worship (vv. 25-26). Furthermore, when they were dinner guests in the home of an unbeliever, they were to eat whatever was placed before them without raising any questions. However, if a fellow-believer were present who took offense at eating meat that had been offered in sacrifice, they were to abstain (vv. 27-29). This was done in deference to the other's conscience.

Paul's final advice in this regard was to do all to the glory of God (v. 31) and to try to avoid offending anyone (v. 32).

Public Worship
11:2 to 14:40

Every church has the privilege of bearing witness to its faith through public services of worship. This is why the congregation needs to be sensitive to the impressions it makes upon the community in which it serves. If unbelievers attend its services, they should find God honored in every aspect of worship. Certainly they should see nothing that would cast reproach upon the gospel.

Now this introduces us to another area in which the Corinthians needed Paul's guidance. Some things were going on there that were causing trouble and discrediting the testimony of the church: (1) Some women were flouting prevailing customs by participating in public worship with uncovered heads (11:2-16). (2) The members were profaning the observance of the Lord's Supper by shameful conduct (11:17-34). (3) Those who spoke in tongues were dividing the church by their exaggerated and erroneous claims regarding their gift (12:1 to 14:40).

Veiling of Women (11:2-16)

Some women in the church at Corinth were creating a disturbance by refusing to wear a veil on their heads. In a Jewish synagogue this would have been regarded as scandalous conduct. Even in some Greek sanctuaries women were supposed to be veiled. Some scholars have claimed that there was a feminist movement in the background. However, it is likely that these Christian women were simply reflecting the more daring styles of the day.

Paul instructed the women to have their heads covered in church. He supported his teaching with the following appeals: (1) *To the order in creation (v. 3).* In the divine order woman comes below man and should wear the head covering as a sign of subjection. (2) *To social custom or propriety (vv. 4-6).* An unveiled woman, like a shorn woman, was looked down upon in disgrace. (3) *To the presence of the angels (v. 10).* We cannot be sure of the meaning of this puzzling reference. Possibly, if men are shocked by the presence of unveiled women in services of worship, how much more the angels! (4) *To nature itself (vv. 13-15).* Nature teaches that long hair is degrading to a man but commendable in a woman. (5) *To the prevailing practice in the churches (v. 16).*

To caricature a passage like this is much easier than to be sensitive to its historical context and enduring sense. Every culture has its social conventions that define acceptable public conduct. Churches do not advance the cause of Christ by outraging them. When a church flouts the prevailing social customs, it offends many of the people to whom it seeks to bear witness. Also, it incurs needless suspicion. But most seriously, it shifts the offense of Christianity from the cross to a mere social convention. It takes a chunk of the periphery and makes it the center.

Observance of the Lord's Supper (11:17-34)

Sometimes a church is worse off for having met together than it would have been had all the members stayed home. That was true in Corinth (v. 17), and the following verses describing the shameful manner in which they observed the Lord's Supper will explain why.

Abuses Associated with Its Observance (11:17-22)

The first abuse that Paul scored was a fractured fellowship: "When you assemble as a church, I hear that there are divisions among you; and I partly believe it" (v. 18). This repeated a similar concern expressed in 1 Corinthians 1:10-12. However, there the divisions derived from conflicting loyalties to different leaders, whereas here they issued from differences in economic and social status. The passage describes the "haves" and the "have-nots" as their relationships were brought to focus in the observance of the Supper. Verse 22 mentions "those who have nothing."

Disorder, gluttony, and drunkenness also characterized the occasion in Corinth. During the common meal that provided the setting for the observance of the Supper, some were not waiting for the others before beginning to eat (v. 21). Perhaps these were the affluent who were more in command of their time than were the laborers and slaves. Furthermore, some were gorging themselves with food and getting drunk, while others were hungry. Thus the poor were humiliated (v. 22). Neither waited for nor provided for, the poor could hardly have regarded the meal as a love feast. No wonder Paul charged, "When you meet together, it is not the Lord's supper that you eat" (v. 20).

Original Meaning of the Supper (11:23-26)

Because of these deplorable circumstances, Paul felt it necessary to remind his readers of the original meaning and purpose of the Lord's Supper. Thus he described for them once more the first Supper, as it had been reported by the earliest Christians. The risen Lord had confirmed it in his own experience (v. 23).

Since the letters of Paul were written before the Gospels, this passage provides our earliest account of the Lord's Supper. Written about AD 54 or 55, this letter brings us within three decades of the event it describes. This feature alone would have assured the importance of 1 Corinthians for all Christians.

"In remembrance of me" (11:23-25).—The original supper had its setting in the dramatic events that moved swiftly toward the death of Jesus on the cross. Paul associated it with the meal that Jesus ate with his desciples "on the night when he was betrayed" (v. 23). He did not specify that it was a Passover meal, though in 1 Corinthians 5:7 he wrote, "For Christ, our paschal lamb, has been sacrificed."

On this solemn occasion Jesus "took bread, and when he had given thanks, he broke it, and said, 'This is my body which is for you. Do this in remembrance of me' " (vv. 23-24). (The marginal reference indicates that some ancient texts read "broken for." This variant is reflected in the KJV.)

You will recall that a lamb was sacrificed on the night of the original Passover in Egypt. (See Ex. 12.) Thereafter the occasion was to be observed as a commemoration of God's deliverance of Israel from bondage. This suggests the context for the meaning of the words Jesus spoke regarding his body. His death on the cross was a sacrifice in our behalf, rendered necessary because of our sins. Through what Jesus Christ did at so great a cost to himself, we may experience the ultimate deliverance, namely, the forgiveness of sins. This is what we are to remember when we partake of the bread that represents his body in the observance of the Lord's Supper.

Paul continued his account in verse 25, "In the same way also the cup, after supper, saying, 'This cup is the new covenant in my blood. Do this, as often as you drink it, in remembrance of me.' "

At this point you need to turn to two Old Testament passages for some pertinent background. First, read Exodus 24:3-8. Observe what Moses did after he had read the law to Israel and had heard their pledge to keep it, "Moses took the blood and threw it upon the people, and said, 'Behold the blood of the covenant which the Lord has made with you in accordance with all these words' " (Ex. 24:8). Thus, the old covenant was sealed with blood. Next, read Jeremiah 31:31-34. Note that this passage promised a new covenant, much greater than the old, "This is the covenant which I will make with the house of Israel after those days, says the Lord: I will put my law within them, and I will write it upon their hearts; and I will be their God, and they shall be my people" (Jer. 31:33). Jesus taught that the cup represented his blood which inaugurated and sealed the new covenant. This is what we are to remember when we partake of it in the observance of the Supper.

How far removed from these sacred meanings of the bread and cup were the disorder and dissension that prevailed in Corinth!

Proclaiming "the Lord's death until he comes" (11:26).—Have you ever thought of the observance of the Lord's Supper as a proclamation? The word translated "proclaim" in verse 26 was used in 1 Corinthians 9:14 to refer to the spoken word. Here it describes *the enacted word.* When a congregation gathers in fellowship at the Lord's table, it proclaims the gospel by its actions, and this proclamation of the Lord's death through the enactments of the Supper is to continue "until he comes." The early Christians lived in the expectancy of the Lord's return.

Thus the observance of the Lord's Supper calls us to remember and proclaim Christ's sacrificial death in our behalf. It invites us to celebrate his living presence. And it fixes our hope upon the victory that will attend his coming.

Need for Self-Examination (11:27-34)

Having described the original meaning and purpose of the Lord's Supper, Paul returned to the deplorable situation in Corinth. He reminded them that anyone who ate the bread or drank the cup in an unworthy manner would be "guilty of profaning the body and blood of the Lord" (11:27). He demanded that each one examine himself in preparation for the observance (v. 28). Otherwise God's judgment would continue to fall upon the congregation: "That is why many of you are weak and ill, and some have died" (v. 30). True self-judgment makes divine judgment unnecessary (v. 31). However, there is both chastening and instruction in God's judgment of his people. His purpose is "that we may not be condemned along with the world" (v. 32).

Paul closed this portion of his instruction by telling the church to wait for one another in the common meal and to satisfy their hunger at home. Other directions could await his coming (11:33-34).

Charismatic Gifts (12:1 to 14:40)

These three chapters provide the most extensive passage in the New Testament on the charismatic gifts. Even these had become a divisive issue in Corinth. Some church members misunderstood them so completely that they regarded their own spiritual gifts with pride and exclusiveness. Also, they tended to place an extreme value on one of the most dramatic of them, namely, speaking in tongues or glossolalia. And the *overclaim* of the glossolalists prompted the *overreaction* of those who did not speak in tongues. The result was further division in a church whose harmony was already disrupted through factions. Thus Paul devoted more space to the problem caused by the glossolalists than any other in the entire letter.

Please observe the pattern of Paul's response to the questions raised by the Corinthians about the problem of glossolalia. First, Paul *taught* about the nature of the church as the body of Christ (12:1-31); next he *appealed* to love as the more excellent way (13:1-13); and only then did he *confront* the glossolalists, who wrongly valued ecstatic utterance above prophetic utterance (14:1-40). We have much to learn from Paul in the very way he sought to resolve this crisis.

Their Nature and Function (12:1-11)

The ultimate test of the presence and power of the Holy Spirit in one's life is the basic confession, "Jesus is Lord" (v. 3). Only the Holy Spirit can plant this confession in a person's heart. Thus a church is the body of Christ, made up of members who have experienced him as Lord.

We are *saved* by grace; we *grow* by grace; and we are *endowed* by grace. From beginning to end the believer's life is an experience of the grace of God.

Enabling graces (12:4-7).—We are no more left to our own resources to be the body of Christ in a community than we are to achieve our own salvation. By grace we are saved, and by the enabling graces or charismatic gifts bestowed by the Holy Spirit upon every believer, we are equipped as a church to serve.

In verses 4-6 Paul mentioned the varieties of spiritual gifts, emphasizing the sameness of their divine source and operation. Then in verse 7 he affirmed, "To each is given the manifestation of the Spirit for the common good." This is great news. It means that every Christian has received some charismatic gift or enabling grace. No one is overlooked. Nor should any believer say, "I cannot do anything meaningful for the Lord." Such a statement reflects upon the competence and generosity of the Holy Spirit.

Moreover, verse 7 teaches that the spiritual gifts are bestowed upon individual members for the good of the entire congregation. They are *functional;* that is, they equip the members of a church to function as the body of Christ in a community. But also they are *congregational*: they are not adornment for our private benefit but rather anointment for our joint services.

No charismatic gift is to be regarded as a merit badge designating God's elite. None is to be regarded as an evidence of total commitment. This is to misunderstand completely the nature and purpose of charismatic endowment. At Corinth some members were so carnal that they tried to make status symbols out of charismatic gifts, especially speaking in tongues.

Enumeration of charismatic gifts (12:8-10).—In verses 8-10 Paul enumerated nine of the charismatic gifts: wisdom, knowledge, faith, gifts of healing, working of miracles, prophecy, the ability to distinguish between spirits, tongues, and the interpretation of tongues. This was a representative, rather than an exhaustive, list. There are other passages in the New Testament which include some charismatic gifts or offices not mentioned here. (See 1 Cor. 7:7; 12:28; Rom. 12:6-8; Eph. 4:11.)

Sovereignty of the Spirit (12:11).—Paul wrote, "All these are inspired by one and the same Spirit, who apportions to each one individually as he wills" (v. 11). Charismatic endowment is not a do-it-yourself kit. Only the Holy Spirit can give these gifts. And if given, how can one boast of any of them as though he has accomplished or attained what he has received?

Their Interdependence (12:12-31)

Baptized into one body (12:12-13).—Throughout the rest of chapter 12 Paul used the analogy of the body to describe a church. A body has many different members and organs; yet all together they form one body. Thus Paul observed, "So it is with Christ. For by one Spirit we were all baptized into one body—Jews or Greeks, slaves or free—and all were made to drink of one Spirit" (12:12-13).

Christians constitute the body of Christ. Through faith in him, prompted by the Spirit, we were baptized into one body. "Made to drink of one Spirit" (12:13) probably designated the receiving of the Spirit at the time of conversion. However, some scholars find here a reference to the Lord's Supper.

As the body of Christ, the church emerges as a new solidarity that transcends all ethnic and social distinctions. (See Gal. 3:27-28; Col. 3:11.)

Folly of discord in the body (12:14-26).—Granted that the church is the body of Christ and that it consists of many members, what shall we make of such discord as prevailed in Corinth? Paul resorted to a method of argument that showed the Corinthians how ridiculous their discord was.

First, he imagined a dissatisfied foot and ear (vv. 15-16). The former wanted to be a hand, and the latter, an eye. Unable to arrange the switch, both declared their intentions to secede from the body. Yet they were no less parts of the body. Fortunately the body is not all eye, ear, or sense of smell (v. 17). "But as it is, God arranged the organs in the body, each one of them, as he chose" (v. 18).

Second, Paul imagined a proud eye and head (v. 21). The former scorned the hand, and the latter, the feet. And yet all parts of the body are united in a remarkable interdependence, and none must be depreciated (vv. 22-26).

The God-appointed ministries of the church (12:27-31).—At this point Paul applied the analogy of the body directly to the church in Corinth, "Now you are the body of Christ and individually members of it" (v. 27). Those who were building a fellowship around the gift of tongues were denying the nature of the church as the body of Christ.

They were making it an association of eyes or noses.

Then Paul cited several whom God had appointed in the church to various ministries: apostles, prophets, teachers, workers of miracles, healers, helpers, administrators, speakers in tongues (v. 28). From the seven rhetorical questions of verses 29-30 we learn that no Christian has all the charismatic gifts, nor is any one gift bestowed upon all.

Verse 31 is transitional, as it points to the more excellent way of love in chapter 13.

Love: The More Excellent Way (13:1-13)

In all religious controversy love is an early casualty. Certainly this was true in Corinth as glossolalists and nonglossolalists squabbled about the relative value of the gift of tongues. Thus Paul found it necessary to emphasize love as the necessary medium for the exercise of all the charismatic gifts. For without love none of the gifts can honor God and build up the church.

Necessity of love (13:1-3).—How important is love? In these verses Paul provided his estimate. All speech, human or angelic, that is not expressed in love is just so much gong-bashing or cymbal-clanging, such as one might hear in a pagan temple. Chances are neither those who prized rhetorical display nor the gift of tongues had thought of this.

And what about "the higher gifts," for example, prophecy, knowledge, and the faith to work miracles? Observe the exaggeration suggested by the recurrence of the word "all" in verse 2. Actually no one could understand *all* mysteries, have *all* knowledge, and have *all* faith. Yet if it were possible and one did not exercise these gifts in love, one would be nothing.

In verse 3 Paul turned from charismatic gifts to deeds normally esteemed by men: charity and martyrdom. What about the man who sells all his possessions and distributes the proceeds to the poor? Or what about the man who gives up his body to be burned? Unless both are done as expressions of love, the answer is the same: he gains nothing.

Characteristic actions of love (13:4-7).—Paul used fifteen verbs in verses 4-7 to describe the characteristic actions of love. From this we learn that the biblical concept of love is dynamic, not static. Love is something you *do.* Unfortunately this fact is weakened by most English translations, which render Paul's strong verbs with "is" and a predicate adjective. For example, Paul wrote, "Love suffers long; love acts kindly" (v. 4). However, the Revised Standard Version reads, "Love is patient and kind." For this reason your author will provide his own translations throughout verses 4-7.

Seven of the characteristic actions of love that Paul enumerated were *positive*: (1) "Love suffers long" (v. 4); (2) "love acts kindly" (v. 4); (3) "it rejoices in the truth" (v. 6); (4) "it bears all things" (v. 7); (5) "it believes all things" (v. 7); (6) "it hopes all things" (v. 7); (7) "it endures all things" (v. 7).

Eight of the typical actions of love that he described were *negative*: (1) "Love does not envy" (v. 4); (2) "love does not boast" (v. 4); (3) "it does not arrogate" or "it is not puffed up" (v. 4); (4) "it does not behave rudely" (v. 5); (5) "it does not seek its own advantage" (v. 5); (6) "it does not act irritably" (v. 5); (7) "it does not keep account of evil" (v. 5); (8) "it does not rejoice in wickedness" (v. 6).

Lest one fault Paul for weighting his description of love's actions negatively, keep in mind the church to which he was writing. The Corinthians needed to be reminded about a lot of things that love did *not* do.

Supremacy of love (13:8-13).—Love is greater than the charismatic gifts, because it is *eternal* and they are *temporal* (vv. 8-12). "Love never ends; as for prophecies, they will pass away; as for tongues, they will cease; as for knowledge, it will pass away" (v. 8).

All the charismatic gifts are divinely bestowed powers or endowments that enable the church to function as the body of Christ during the present age. This is the time between the resurrection and the return of Jesus Christ. Beyond this, there will no longer be any need for the Holy Spirit to bestow them.

In verse 11 Paul continued his contrast between the imperfection of the present age and the perfection of the future by his analogy of human growth. And in verse 12 he reinforced it by his analogy of the mirror. Our knowledge of God at the present time may be compared to the imperfect reflection of an ancient metal mirror. However, in the eternal order our knowledge of God will be "face to face." Partial knowledge will yield to a full understanding of God, even as we have been fully understood by him.

Throughout verses 8-12 the comparison has been between the *temporality* of the charismatic gifts and the *eternality* of love.

Parenthetically, two present-day misconceptions need to be dealt with here: (1) Some press the meaning of the verb translated "they will cease" in verse 8 to support the conclusion that the Holy Spirit has not bestowed the gift of tongues since the end of the apostolic age. However, this reads into the verb form more than is there, as the study of any standard translation will show. (2) Some find in verse 10, "when the perfect comes, the imperfect will pass away," a reference to the closing of the canon. Presumably Paul taught that once the canon was completed, the Holy Spirit would no longer bestow certain charismatic gifts, including the gift of tongues. But to inject canonical considerations into Paul's instruction of the Corinthians is remarkably farfetched. Perhaps both of these proposals owe more to dogmatic concerns than to either exegetical or historical insights.

Unlike the temporal charismatic gifts, there are certain great realities that will endure forever (v. 13). These are faith, hope, and love—a magnificent triad. (Compare 1 Thess. 1:3; 5:8; Gal. 5:5-6; Rom. 5:1-5; Col. 1:4-5.)

All three abide forever: *faith,* because our relationship to God will always be one of trust and commitment; *hope,* because we will participate with God in an eternal order that is dynamic; and *love,* because where God is, love is.

And of these three, love is the greatest!

The Priority of Prophecy (14:1-40)

In chapter 14 Paul confronted the erroneous claims of the glossolalists directly. He did it by comparing the relative values of two speaking gifts: prophecy and speaking in tongues.

Prophecy is Holy Spirit-inspired utterance that is intelligible. That is, it has a recognizable vocabulary, grammar, and syntax through which God's message can be communicated.

On the other hand, speaking in tongues is Holy Spirit-inspired utterance that is not intelligible. It is a form of ecstatic utterance. Observe the following evidences in support of this conclusion: (1) It is addressed to God, not to men. Those who hear the glossolalist cannot understand him, for "he utters mysteries in the Spirit" (v. 2). (2) Not even the glossolalist understands what he is saying; thus he is urged to "pray for the power to interpret" (v. 13). (3) While speaking in tongues, the mind and utterance are not coordinated as in ordinary speech: the "mind is unfruitful" (v. 14). (4) Glossolalia is a medium for expressing praise or thanksgiving to God (vv. 16-17). (5) The glossolalist can control the exercise of his gift. Otherwise there would be no point in Paul's command for him to remain silent in church in the absense of an interpreter (v. 28).

Glossolalia is *not* the ability to speak in foreign languages. One has only to assume this meaning long enough to insert it in every pertinent reference in chapter 14 to discover its inadequacy. The contexts simply do not support this sense.

Prophecy more important than tongues (14:1-25).—Both prophecy and speaking in tongues are valid charismatic gifts, but they are by no means of equal importance in the ministries of the church. Whereas the glossolalists regarded their gift more highly than all other gifts, Paul claimed that prophecy was more important. He gave the following reasons:

(1) *Because prophecy edifies the whole church (14:1-12).*—There is a value to glossolalia, as one rightly expects of any gift bestowed by the Holy Spirit. Overreacting nonglossolalists of any age do violence to the plain teaching of 1 Corinthians 12—14 when they deny either its validity or worth. They may do this severely, even blasphemously, by alleging: "It's of the devil!" They may do it smugly, by relegating it to the neurotic fringe of Christian discipleship. Or they may do it summarily by declaring that the Holy Spirit has not bestowed it since the apostolic age. This seems to be an encroachment upon the sovereignty of the Holy Spirit, who alone determines the *whom, what, when,* and *where* of all his gifts (v. 11).

However, in Corinth, and often since, glossolalia was magnified all out of proportion to its value. Self-edification is its primary contribution. Unless accompanied by the gift of interpretation, it cannot build up the congregation (v. 5). But prophecy is different. As glossolalia is ecstatic speech addressed to God by men, so prophecy is intelligible speech addressed from God through men to men. Paul claimed, "He who speaks in a tongue edifies himself, but he who prophesies edifies the church" (v. 4).

(2) *Because prophecy can be understood by all (14:13-19).*—The one who is praising God in tongues may be expressing genuine thanks, but another will not even be able to know when an "Amen" would be appropriate (v. 16). For this reason Paul stated, "I thank God that I speak in tongues more than you all; nevertheless, in church I would rather speak five words with my mind, in order to instruct others, than ten thousand words in a tongue" (vv. 18-19).

Paul claimed that he spoke in tongues. This should keep nonglossolalists from denying the validity of this gift. Yet as a glossolalist, Paul placed greater value upon five instructional words in church than upon literally myriads or countless words in a tongue. This should keep glossolalists from exaggerating the value of this gift.

(3) *Because prophecy inspires conviction, confession, and worship (14:20-25).*—In this passage Paul contrasted the impressions made upon unbelievers by glossolalia and prophecy. According to verse 23 glossolalia invited scorn: "If, therefore, the whole church assembles and all speak in tongues, and outsiders or unbelievers enter, will they not say that you are mad?" On the other hand, prophecy inspired worship: "But if all prophesy, and an unbeliever or outsider enters, he is convicted by all, he is called to account by all, the secrets of his heart are disclosed; and so, falling on his face, he will worship God and declare that God is really among you" (vv. 24-25).

How different the responses of the unbelievers in these two scenes of public worship! Surely the gift of prophecy that prompts them to worship God is vastly superior to the gift of tongues that leads them to say scornfully, "You are crazy!"

Practical Guidance in Worship (14:26-40)

A brief summary must suffice here. Having stressed the greater importance of prophecy to glossolalia in verses 1-25, Paul devoted the rest of the chapter, verses 26-40, to practical instructions in public worship. In verses 26, 33, and 40 he laid down the broad principles that must prevail in all the worship services. And throughout the rest of the passage he dealt with such specific items as: (1) the proper exercise of charismatic gifts (v. 26); (2) the number of glossolalists or prophets who may take part in any one service (vv. 27-32), (3) the restrictions upon the participation of women (v. 33-36).

Resurrection

15:1-58

In this magnificent chapter of Christian hope we have the earliest existing account of the resurrection of Jesus Christ. Written within three decades of the event it describes, it bears powerful testimony to the resurrection as the central affirmation of the Christian faith.

Yet in Corinth some were saying that there was no resurrection of the dead (v. 12). Due to the lack of information, we cannot be certain of the exact nature of the Corinthian denial. Possibly it recoiled from the

Jewish belief in a resurrected body, while affirming a Greek emphasis upon the immortality of the soul. (See Acts 17:32.) Or possibly it reflected the gnostic tendency to exaggerate the emphasis upon the present resurrection existence of the believer, while rejecting the hope of a future bodily resurrection. Earlier Paul had rebuked the arrogant Corinthians for acting as though the consummation had already occurred and they were basking in its glories (4:8-13).

At any rate Paul sought to refute the denial of the resurrection in a lengthy chapter, in which he affirmed the certainty of the resurrection (15:1-34) and discussed the nature of the resurrected body (15:35-58).

Certainty of the Resurrection (15:1-34)

Testimony of Eyewitnesses (15:1-11)

There were three vital emphases in the gospel message as it had been delivered to Paul: (1) "Christ died for our sins in accordance with the scriptures" (v. 3). This affirmed the saving significance of Christ's death on the cross. (Compare Rom. 3:21-26; Gal. 3:13-14; 2 Cor. 5:18-21.) (2) "He was buried" (v. 4). This underscored the reality of his death. (3) "He was raised on the third day in accordance with the scriptures" (v. 4). This constituted the completion of God's redemptive act through Jesus Christ. Not until the death and burial gave way to the resurrection triumph over sin and death did we have a gospel. There is evidence of an early confession of faith in these verses.

Following his resurrection from the dead, Jesus Christ appeared to several of his followers.

He appeared to Cephas, or Peter (v. 5). For references in the gospels in this connection, turn to Luke 24:34; Mark 16:7; and John 21:1-14.

He appeared to the twelve (v. 5). Pertinent passages may be found in Matthew 28:16-20; Luke 24:36-49; and John 20:19-25. Of course, he never appeared to Judas Iscariot. In the last named passage Thomas was absent.

He appeared to more than five hundred brethren at one time (v. 6). Paul is the only source for this appearance. He stated that most of this number still survived.

He appeared to James (v. 7). This likely refers to the Lord's brother, who became prominent in the Jerusalem church. (See Acts 15:13-21.) Again, no such appearance is described in the Gospels.

He appeared to all the apostles (v. 7). This may have been the appearance to the apostles when Thomas was present, described in John 20:26-29. Or it may have been at the time of the ascension recorded in Luke 24:50-53; Acts 1:9-11.

Paul climaxed his list of resurrection appearances by writing, "Last of all, as to one untimely born, he appeared also to me" (v. 8). He included himself among those to whom the risen Lord had appeared.

Denial of the Resurrection (15:12-19)

Now Paul was ready to challenge the Corinthian denial of the resurrection of the dead more directly. He did not indicate whether it included a denial of the resurrection of Christ. Probably it did not. However, in Paul's argument the denial of the resurrection of the dead constituted a denial of the Lord's resurrection, "If there is no resurrection of the dead, then Christ has not been raised" (15:13; see 15:16).

For the sake of argument in this passage Paul assumed that Christ had not been raised. Then he proceeded to draw the conclusions that inevitably followed upon the false premise. If Christ has not been raised, Paul said that we would have: (1) *Preaching without truth,* "our preaching is in vain" (v. 14). Worse than that! An unresurrected Christ would have made a false witness out of Paul (v. 15). (2) *Faith without forgiveness,* "your faith is futile and you are still in your sins" (v. 17). Had Christ remained the victim of sin and death following his crucifixion, he could not have delivered us from their power. A dead Christ is no deliverer! (3) *Death without hope,* "Then those also who have fallen asleep in Christ have perished" (v. 18). The death of those who have confessed Christ as Savior has the same end as the death of those who have denied him. (4) *Sacrifice without meaning,* "If for this life only we have hoped in Christ, we are of all men most to be pitied" (v. 19). For the nobility of the sacrifice was wasted upon an illusion.

Consequences of Christ's Resurrection (15:20-28)

At this point Paul seemed unable to restrain himself any longer. Having listed the somber conclusions that would follow upon the premise of an unresurrected Christ, he turned the argument completely around with a mighty affirmation of faith. Christ has been raised from the dead, and he has become "the first fruits of those who have fallen asleep" (v. 20).

Leviticus 23:4-11 provides the background for the metaphor of the firstfruits. The waving of the sheaf of the firstfruits of the grain harvest before the Lord served to consecrate the whole harvest to follow.

Similarly the resurrection of Christ as the firstfruits of those who have died becomes the assurance that all who trust him shall have a resurrection like his.

The same resurrection hope is assured in the Adam-Christ analogy in verses 21-22, "For as by a man came death, by a man has come also the resurrection of the dead. For as in Adam all die, so also in Christ shall all be made alive." As Adam was the medium of death, so Christ is the medium of life.

But there are orders in the resurrection: Christ is the firstfruits, "then at his coming those who belong to Christ" (v. 23). The resurrection of believers is related to the second coming of Christ. "Then comes the end, when he delivers the kingdom to God the Father after destroying every rule and every authority and power" (v. 24). And death, described as the last enemy, will be destroyed also (v. 26).

Other Arguments for the Resurrection (15:29-34)

Assuming for the sake of argument that there was no resurrection, Paul drew two more negative conclusions: (1) *Baptism in behalf of the dead is futile.* "If the dead are not raised at all, why are people baptized on their behalf?" (v. 29). This puzzling verse has attracted a wider range of rescue efforts than almost any other in the entire letter. The most obvious meaning is vicarious baptism; that is, baptism in the place of another who died unbaptized. But this is alien to the teaching on baptism in the rest of the New Testament. Some have suggested that the passage describes the subsequent conversion and baptism of one for whom a deceased relative or friend had formerly prayed. This is comfortable, but the passage remains hard to understand. (2) *Risking one's life for the sake of the gospel is folly,* "Why am I in peril every hour?" (v. 30). It is doubtful that Paul's statement about having fought "with beasts at Ephesus" is to be taken literally of an experience in the arena (v. 32). More likely it was Paul's way of describing vividly the great dangers that he encountered in his missionary work. (See 2 Cor. 11:23-33.) If the dead are not raised, pagan abandon and despair have their own dreary logic (v. 32).

Nature of the Resurrected Body (15:35-58)

Two questions begin this passage, "Some one will ask, 'How are the dead raised? With what kind of body do they come?' " (v. 35). The first implies the *impossibility* of the resurrection, and the second implies its *inconceivability.* To the first question Paul devoted little attention. Earlier he had written, "God raised the Lord and will also raise us up by his power" (6:14). But to the second question about the nature of the resurrected body he gave a careful answer.

Analogy from Nature (15:36-44)

The point that Paul intended in his analogy from nature was that death is a transition to a higher form of life. A seed is planted in the ground; it dies (germinates); and it yields a body of God's choosing (v. 38). And great variety prevails. Men, animals, birds, and fish have different kinds of flesh, each well suited to its particular environment (v. 39).

Not only are there differences among earthly bodies but also between celestial and terrestrial bodies (v. 40). Some scholars regard these celestial bodies as heavenly beings. And certainly among the heavenly bodies—sun, moon, and stars—there are differences in glory (v. 41).

With what splendid variety and adequacy God has clothed all forms of celestial and terrestrial life in the present order! Surely such a God will not be hard pressed to provide suitable bodies for all who share in his eternal order.

In the application of the seed metaphor Paul wrote, "So it is with the resurrection of the dead. What is sown is perishable, what is raised is imperishable. It is sown in dishonor, it is raised in glory. It is sown in weakness, it is raised in power. It is sown a physical body, it is raised a spiritual body" (vv. 42-44).

Appeal to Scripture (15:45-50)

Throughout this discussion Paul has been answering the question about the nature of the resurrected body. And in the preceding verse he had stated that it was a *spiritual body,* "If there is a physical body, there is also a spiritual body" (v. 44).

Now Paul appealed to the Scriptures to support and expand his conclusion, "Thus it is written, 'The first man Adam became a living being;' the last Adam became a life-giving spirit" (v. 45). The first part of the verse was a quotation of Genesis 2:7 with some modifications, but the last half was Paul's comment.

The first Adam was a man of dust. From our relationship to him we have a physical body. But the last Adam (or second man) is from heaven. From our relationship to him we will have a spiritual body (vv.

47-48). "Just as we have borne the image of the man of dust, we shall also bear the image of the man of heaven" (v. 49). Thus the spiritual body that Christians will have in the resurrection will be similar to the body of the risen Lord.

This is necessary, because "flesh and blood cannot inherit the kingdom of God, nor does the perishable inherit the imperishable" (v. 50).

Triumph over Death (15:51-58)

In one of the most exalted passages in the New Testament Paul described the glorious consummation of the kingdom of God. Since the eternal order is not one of flesh and blood, all believers must undergo a change at the time of the Lord's return (v. 51). Those whose death has preceded his appearing will be resurrected, and those who survive until he comes will be transformed (vv. 52-54). When this comes to pass, the ancient hope will be fulfilled, "Death is swallowed up in victory" (v. 54; see Isa. 25:8).

Now it is time to taunt death. For in verse 55 Paul phrased a taunt song, much after the fashion of Hosea 13:14.

In verse 56 Paul explained that the sting of death was sin, and that the power of sin was the law. Sin constitutes death's sting and evokes our greatest fears of it. Unforgiven sin, the summation of a lifelong rebellion against God, causes our fear of death. For the prospect of standing unprepared before God in judgment is foreboding indeed.

But it need not be this way. The God who loves all men has moved through the life, death, and resurrection of his Son to provide the forgiveness that reconciles us to him in loving response forever.

Hear Paul's burst of praise, "Thanks be to God, who gives us the victory through our Lord Jesus Christ" (v. 57).

Conclusion
16:1-24

Relief Offering (16:1-4)

Galatians 2:10 provides the earliest reference to the proposed offering for the poor Christians in Jerusalem. The leaders there had urged Paul and Barnabas to remember the poor, and Paul had expressed an eagerness to comply with the request.

This passage reveals that Paul was true to his promise. Evidently the Corinthians had heard about his instructions to the churches of Galatia and had written to him about their own participation in the offering (v. 1). In these verses Paul responded to their inquiry with some specific guidance.

At least five principles of Christian giving may be discerned in the passage:(1) *It was inclusive (v. 2)*. Each one in the congregation was to have a part in the offering. (2) *It was systematic*. "On the first day of every week, each of you is to put something aside and store it up" (v. 2). (3) *It was proportionate (v. 2)*. As one had prospered, so he was to give. (4) *It was voluntary (v. 2)*. In the Jewish system a Temple tax was levied annually upon every male twenty years of age and over. There is no evidence that Paul was attempting to adapt this practice to the Gentile congregations in behalf of the mother church in Jerusalem. (5) *It was administered wisely (v. 3)*. Delegates appointed by the churches would take the gift to Jerusalem. And if advisable, Paul was prepared to go, too (v. 4).

Travel Plans (16:5-9)

Paul stated his intention to visit the Corinthians, taking the overland route through Macedonia rather than sailing directly from Ephesus (v. 5). He was eager to spend some time with them, perhaps even the entire winter, rather than to make a brief visit (vv. 6-7). Then they would be able to send him on his way, wherever he might go. Paul did not disclose any travel plans beyond his visit to Corinth at this time.

However, he did say that he would stay in Ephesus until Pentecost (v. 8). This was the great Jewish feast that followed seven weeks after Passover. His reason for doing so was to take advantage of the outstanding opportunity to preach the gospel there (v. 9). But there were many adversaries.

An open door with adversaries and a closed door look very much alike.

Final Appeals and Farewell (16:10-24)

Paul mentioned Timothy's forthcoming visit to Corinth and urged the church to receive him as one committed to the Lord's work (vv. 10-11). Apollos had not been able to come to them, but would when he had opportunity (v. 12).

Paul counseled the church, "Be watchful, stand firm in your faith, be courageous, be strong. Let all that you do be done in love" (v. 13).

Next he paid a tribute to the household of Stephanas for their faithful service (v. 15). Such men were worthy of their recognition and respect as leaders (v. 16).

Thanks were expressed to the church for the coming of Stephanas, Fortunatus, and Achaicus (vv. 17-18). They likely brought to Paul the letter from Corinth, to which he gave answer in this letter. Moreover they probably carried 1 Corinthians to the church.

Asian churches sent their greetings, with special mention of Aquila and Priscilla, beloved by many in Corinth (vv. 19-20).

Then Paul took the pen from his amanuensis or secretary, to bring his letter to a close (v. 21). Other letters reveal that this was his custom (Gal. 6:11; 2 Thess. 3:17; Col. 4:18; Philem. 19). His final words were, "If any one has no love for the Lord, let him be accursed. Our Lord, come! The grace of the Lord Jesus be with you. My love be with you all in Christ Jesus. Amen" (vv. 22-24).

BIBLIOGRAPHY

Romans

Barclay, William. *The Letter to the Romans.* Rev. ed. The Daily Study Bible Series. Philadelphia: The Westminster Press, 1975.

Barrett, C. K. *A Commentary on the Epistle to the Romans.* Harper's New Testament Commentaries. New York: Harper and Brothers, Publishers, 1957.

Best, Ernest. *The Letter of Paul to the Romans.* The Cambridge Bible Commentary. Cambridge: At the University Press, 1967.

Black, Matthew. *Romans.* New Century Bible. Greenwood, S. C.; The Attic Press, Inc., 1973.

Bruce, F. F. *The Epistle of Paul to the Romans.* The Tyndale New Testament Commentaries. Grand Rapids, Michigan: Wm. B. Eerdmans Publishing Company, 1963.

Brunner, Emil. *The Letter to the Romans.* Translated by H. A. Kennedy. Philadelphia: The Westminster Press, 1959.

Cranfield, C. E. B. *A Critical and Exegetical Commentary on the Epistle to the Romans.* The International Critical Commentary. 6th ed. 2 vols. Edinburgh: T. & T. Clark, Ltd., 1975.

Dodd, C. H. *The Epistle of Paul to the Romans.* The Moffatt New Testament Commentary. New York: Harper and Brothers Publishers, n.d.

Hunter, A. M. *The Epistle to the Romans.* The Torch Bible Commentaries. London: SCM Press Ltd., 1955.

Manson, T. W. *Romans.* Peake's Commentary on the Bible. Edited by Matthew Black and H. H. Rowley. London: Thomas Nelson and Sons Ltd., 1962.

Moody, Dale. *Romans.* The Broadman Bible Commentary. Vol. 10. Nashville, Tennessee: Broadman Press, 1970.

Murray, John. *The Epistle to the Romans.* The New International
Commentary on the New Testament. Grand Rapids, Michigan:
Wm. B. Eerdmans Publishing Co., 1968.

Nygren, Anders. *Commentary on Romans.* Translated by Carl C.
Rasmussen. Philadelphia: Muhlenberg Press, 1949.

Smart, James D. *Doorway to a New Age.* Philadelphia: The Westminster Press, 1972.

Taylor, Vincent. *The Epistle to the Romans.* Epworth Preacher's
Commentaries. London: The Epworth Press, 1955.

Vaughan, Curtis and Corley, Bruce. *Romans: A Study Guide Commentary.* Grand Rapids, Michigan: Zondervan Publishing House, 1976.

1 Corinthians

Baird, William. *The Corinthian Church —A Biblical Approach to
Urban Culture.* New York: Abingdon Press, 1964.

Barclay, William. *The Letters to the Corinthians.* Rev. ed. The Daily
Study Bible Series. Philadelphia. The Westminster Press, 1975.

Barrett, C. K. *The First Epistle to the Corinthians.* Harper's New
Testament Commentaries. New York: Harper & Row, Publishers,
1968.

Brown, Raymond B. *1 Corinthians. The Broadman Bible Commentary.*
Vol. 10. Nashville, Tennessee: Broadman Press, 1970.

Craig, Clarence T. and Short, John. *First Corinthians.* The Interpreter's Bible. Vol. X. New York: Abingdon-Cokesbury Press, 1953.

Hering, Jean. *The First Epistle of Saint Paul to the Corinthians.*
London: The Epworth Press, 1962.

Moffatt, James. *The First Epistle of Paul to the Corinthians.* The Moffatt New Testament Commentary. New York: Harper and Brothers
Publishers, n.d.

Morris, Leon. *The First Epistle of Paul to the Corinthians.* The Tyndale
New Testament Commentaries. Grand Rapids, Michigan: Wm. B.
Eerdmans Publishing Company, 1958.

Robertson, Archibald and Plummer, Alfred. *A Critical and Exegetical
Commentary on the First Epistle of St. Paul to the Corinthians.* The
International Critical Commentary. Edinburgh: T. & T. Clark,
1914.

Thrall, Margaret E. *The First and Second Letters of Paul to the Corinthians.* The Cambridge Bible Commentary. Cambridge: At the University Press, 1965.